LET'S COOK INTERNATIONAL

THE CANADIAN RED CROSS SOCIETY

Canadian Cataloguing in Publication Data

Let's Cook International
1. Cookery, International
2. Canadian Red Cross Society
British Columbia/Yukon Division

TX 725.A1L48 1986 641.59 C84-091498-9

ISBN #0-920581-02-1

Published by:

The Canadian Red Cross Society,
B.C./Yukon Division,
4750 Oak Street
Vancouver, B.C. V6H 2N9

Printed by: Hignell Printing Ltd., Winnipeg, Manitoba
Book Design: Chris Bergthorsen, Embryo Communications Ltd.
Illustrations: Kathryn E. Shoemaker
Cover Photograph: Frank Grundig
Typesetting: Domino-Link Graphic Communications Ltd.

Distributed by **Gordon Soules Book Publishers Ltd.** • 1359 Ambleside Lane, West Vancouver, BC, Canada V7T 2Y9 • PMB 620, 1916 Pike Place #12, Seattle, WA 98101-1097 US
E-mail: books@gordonsoules.com
Web site: http://www.gordonsoules.com
(604) 922 6588 Fax: (604) 688 5442

Acknowledgements

The Canadian Red Cross Society wishes to say a very special thank you to all those who gave so freely of their time and expertise to make this book possible, especially to

Chris Bergthorsen for the book design,
Kathryn E. Shoemaker for the illustrations,
Frank Grundig for the cover photograph,
Jennifer Pike for the menu write-ups,
Jack Hignell, our printer,
Zenith Graphics for the colour separations,

and Janet Sutherland, Eileen Wilson, Ann Hockey, Frances Barr, Joy McLelland, Sheila Rogers, Vicki Clarke, Ken Jackson, Judy Lashley, Donna Shandro, Donna Anderson, Gordon Soules, and to over 30 testers and countless tasters and many others who gave so much help and advice.

Merne Bruchet, Cookbook Co-ordinator
Sharon Slutsky, Financial/Marketing Co-ordinator
Wendy Affleck, Food Editor
Margaret Hyslop, Staff Liaison

Introduction

The Canadian Red Cross Society is part of the great international League of Red Cross Societies. In times of peace or war it is dedicated to the improvement of health, the prevention of disease, and the mitigation of suffering throughout the world.

This cookbook represents the international nature of the organization, as well as being a new form of fund raising for the Canadian Red Cross Society.

Letters were sent to member nations, asking them to share with us their menus for a festive meal; dishes that best typify the cuisine of their country that they might serve to foreign visitors. We received a wonderful response, so the monumental task of testing and tasting began. While trying to retain the authenticity of the original recipes, they were adapted wherever necessary to North American tastes and cooking techniques.

Let's Cook International is divided into two parts. The first section contains menus from countries and regions of the world, with a special focus on Canadian cuisine. Our recipe section is arranged in conventional order, from starters through to desserts. We have also included additional recipes that do not form part of our main menus, but were just too good to leave out.

So we invite you to join us on our culinary journey — Let's Cook International. We hope you enjoy this book.

TABLE OF CONTENTS

Menus

Africa

DINNER FOR 6

Pumpkin Fritters – Botswana p.50
Nsomba Mangochi Lake Fish – Malawi p.70
Gages – Sierra Leone p.113
Coconut Cream Pie – Liberia p.165

Tropical fruits and vegetables are the mainstay of the African diet, with nuts and grains providing the necessary protein. The ubiquitous peanut, along with maize, was brought to Africa by the Portuguese from South America in the 16th century as a cheap food for slaves being shipped to the New World.

Maize is cultivated everywhere; no wild maize has ever been found — and mealie meal, a thick porridge made from finely ground maize, is a staple African dish. Coconut palms are found along all tropical shores. The nuts float and take root where they wash up. As well as providing refreshing drinks from the green nut, and the grated coconut meat we know from the dried nuts, the palm has many other uses for the African people. It provides "thatched" roofs, shelters and matting, and is even used as an ingredient in margarine. Starchy vegetables such as yams and cassava, and many kinds of bananas and plantains grow in Africa. Plantains may either be used green — boiled and mashed into a "fou-fou" — or ripened until their skins are black and the fruit soft. Peel, slice and fry them in butter, and serve sprinkled with brown sugar and lime juice.

Citrus fruit also grow in abundance in some parts of Africa, and we have included among our recipes a delicious grapefruit spread from Botswana.

Australia

DINNER FOR 6

Easy-going, casual, friendly, are words that best describe the Australian people. Their culinary tastes are simple, and are little influenced by the more sophisticated cuisine of Europe. Plain "meat and two veg" is the favourite meal, washed down inevitably with beer. It is said that Australians tend to rank their cities and towns by the relative merits of their beer rather than by civic standards.

Beef is favoured over lamb (it seems those zillion sheep are raised mainly for their famous Australian wool) and is often overdone by North American standards. Never mind! Try our carpet bag steak as something different and uniquely Australian.

Another Australian specialty is the superb Pavlova. Various claims are made as to its origin, but one story has it that a chef in Perth, Western Australia, created this spectacular dessert in 1919 to honour the visiting prima ballerina, Anna Pavlova.

Despite the proliferation of breweries, Australian wine is now making its mark on world markets. Hock, reisling, chablis, burgundy and claret wines are of excellent quality and have become big business.

Austria

DINNER FOR 6

Liptauer Cheese p.42
Veal Escalope p.106
Buttered Noodles p.127
Carrots in White Wine p.116
Sachertorte p.173

The Hapsburg dynasty ruled the great Austrian empire for the better part of the last five centuries. Its power and influence spread throughout central Europe, as far north as the Netherlands and even west to Spain. Vienna was the centre of culture, of music and the arts, and of culinary feats worthy of the royal court. Austria adopted the best of Central European cuisine as its own, and Bavarian dumplings, Hungarian goulash and Italian noodles feature in Austrian meals to this day. Even the famed Wiener Schnitzel had its origins as an Italian veal dish. Among the delicacies created by Austrian chefs themselves are chicken stuffed with goose liver and madeira, Dobosh (a multi-layered cake with chocolate filling), and the famed Sachertorte. This rich dark chocolate cake, filled with apricot jam, was so highly prized that two establishments battled in court for seven years for the right to call the recipe their own. In fact everywhere in Austria you will find a wonderful array of strudels and pastries of all kinds, often embellished with schlagzahne (whipped cream), and served with strong, dark coffee.

Austria today is a small country, with beautiful cities and many charming Tyrolean towns and villages. It is thickly forested, and mountaineering and skiing are popular pastimes. What better meal after a day in the mountains than our hearty Veal Escalope served with noodles and vegetables and finished off with Sachertorte!

Belgium

LUNCH FOR 6

Flemish Waterzooi p.80
Diplomate p.152

Belgium has two main population groups: the Flemings in the north, and the Walloons in the south. Despite differences of language and temperament, Belgians are united in their love of good food.

Waterzooi falls somewhere between a soup and a stew, and can be made either from fish or from chicken. The people of Ghent are said to make the best fish Waterzooi, and the chicken variety is a specialty of Brussels. Whatever the main ingredient, it is thickened with eggs and cream and served in a deep soup bowl.

Vegetables are highly esteemed in Belgium. Malines asparagus, for example, is prized, as is the endive, and salads are popular. Potatoes almost always accompany meat dishes. The Belgians are very fond of fried potatoes — "frites" — and they are eaten any time.

Diplomate dessert is rich and delicious, made with custard and ladyfingers. Satisfying enough for anyone's sweet tooth, it is served in homes everywhere in Belgium.

Alberta

DINNER FOR 6

Tangy Alberta Shortribs p.94
Cheesey Potatoes p.121
Spinach and Mushroom Salad p.61
Rhubarb Strawberry Fantasy p.158

Although school books used to describe Alberta as a land of enormous wheatfields, cattle ranching is important to this province, as is the sugar beet crop. And of course the discovery of oil has meant that the economy no longer has to rely on agriculture alone. Tourism is also a big industry in the Rockies, with beautiful resorts such as Banff and Lake Louise.

The mountains screen Alberta from the moderating influence of the Pacific Ocean, but sometimes in cold midwinter a flow of warm, dry air — the Chinook — will arrive unexpectedly and cause the temperature to rise about twenty degrees in just a few hours.

Pioneer settlers found life hard in Alberta, and it was difficult for them to grow many of the crops they were used to. However, rhubarb, a perennial vegetable which originally came from Mongolia, survives the winters well. Wild strawberries also grow on the prairie; people used to gather the leaves of the plant for brewing into a tea which was thought to be good for sore throats, and other ailments.

British Columbia and Yukon

DINNER FOR 6

Pacific Shrimp Sauté p.46
Armstrong Cheddar Cheese Balls p.43
Barbecued Salmon with
Wild Rice Stuffing p.69
Marinated Vegetables p.65
Clearbrook Raspberry Soufflé p.162
Lulu Island Cranberry Cooler p.66

Half of British Columbia's population lives on the Lower Mainland of the province, where snow is rare and the inhabitants tend toward a certain smugness about the temperate climate. The flip side of the coin though, is the heavy rainfall, which causes some outsiders to maintain that British Columbians don't tan, they rust instead. However, Canada's westernmost province, with its miles of Pacific coastline, spectacular mountains and valleys and desert-like region, is fortunate in having many different types of climate, thereby enabling just about anything to be grown or raised.

Everything on our menu is home-grown: there is a thriving cheese industry in the central interior of the province; Pacific salmon is famous the world over; and the tiny Pacific shrimp is available fresh during many months of the year. Ninety-five percent of Canada's cranberry crop comes from the peat bogs of the Fraser River delta, and a huge variety of other fruits and vegetables are grown on the Lower Mainland and in the Okanagan Valley, which exports large quantities of fruit.

Manitoba

DINNER FOR 6

Perogies p.128
Borscht p.50
Tossed Green Salad
Vinaterta p.175

The cooking of Manitoba reflects many influences: Ukrainian, Mennonite, Icelandic, Jewish, German and Scottish. Most of the prairie pioneers stuck close to their homes because of the bitter winter weather and long distances between settlements, and a strong interest in the kitchen resulted.

Mennonites settled the province in the nineteenth century. They came originally from Germany, but stopped over in Russia for about a hundred and fifty years before coming to Canada. The Ukrainian influence is strong, too; large numbers of Ukrainians emigrated to western Canada around the turn of the century — hence our recipe for perogies. Borscht is the national soup of both Russia and Poland. You can make it thick or thin, serve it hot or cold, and it need not necessarily contain beetroot. However, it is always served with a sour cream garnish.

It is said that more Icelanders live in Manitoba than in Reykjavik, Iceland's capital. They settled there after erupting volcanoes had devasted their country. Vinaterta is an Icelandic specialty; several layers of rich pastry, filled with fruit and covered with almond icing.

New Brunswick

DINNER FOR 6

Clam Pie p.74
Fiddleheads with
Bacon and Cheese Sauce p.120
Baked Apple Dumplings p.144

Fishing is vital to the New Brunswick economy — lobster, crab, clams and tuna being just some of the harvest. Farming is mixed, and mainly for local markets. There is a variety of fresh fruit and vegetables, especially potatoes.

Legend has it that when the Archangel Gabriel stepped aside to let Adam and Eve out of Eden, he brushed his wings against a boulder, a feather dropped, took root, and the fiddlehead fern was born. There are differing stories about how the fiddlehead got its name. Some say it came from the tightly curled top which is shaped like the end of a violin, others say it is a nautical term for a scroll shape in place of a figurehead on a ship. Whatever the truth, they are the young fronds of the ostrich fern and a New Brunswick delicacy. The settlers copied the Malacite Indians of the area and used the fiddleheads for food.

The first European settlers were French — Acadians — and the province still has a large French-speaking population. An Acadian cooking speciality is Poutine à Trou, or apple dumpling, which is unique to New Brunswick.

Newfoundland

DINNER FOR 6

Fish and Tomato Scallop p.76
Newfoundland Biscuits p.135
Fresh Broccoli Salad 61
Blueberry Cobbler p.148

Newfoundland's past, is anything but dull, even though one disenchanted early visitor described it as a "land of fogs, bogs and dogs". It is claimed that the distinctive Newfoundland accent and vocabulary bear a close resemblance to that of British seamen about three hundred years ago, and this may be true, since before the middle of the sixteenth century fishing ships from England and Ireland had come over to work the Banks.

Although when Newfoundlanders speak of "fish" they mean cod, other types are harvested too, such as haddock, halibut, turbot, salmon, sole and herring. Newfoundlanders tend to like their food salty, and the provincial dish is the "boiled dinner": salt beef or pork with cabbage, potato and turnip. These popular vegetables grow well in this rocky land.

One settler's recollection of past cold winters in Newfoundland was of wrapping up the bread at night and placing it snugly under the covers at the foot of the bed in order to prevent it from freezing.

Northwest Territories

DINNER FOR 6

Roast Caribou p.94
Wild Cranberry Sauce p.138
Northern Vegetables p.114
Bannock p.135
Spence Bay Coffee-Rum Sauce with Ice Cream p.180
Dried Fruit and Nuts

The Northwest Territories cover one third of Canada, yet because of the long, northern winters the population numbers only about 45,000. Mining is the mainstay of the economy, although traditionally the fur trade dominated and remains important.

The caribou, a relative of the reindeer, has for centuries been a main source of food, clothing and shelter for the Inuit and the Indians. The Inuit people, who extend from Greenland to Alaska and Siberia, have their own traditions and language (they have one hundred different words for various types of snow), live mainly in coastal areas, and hunt and fish.

Since only the southern part of the Mackenzie district is outside the permafrost area, almost all foodstuffs for northerners must be brought in from the warmer parts of Canada. A few vegetables can be raised in the short growing season near the capital, Yellowknife, and some berries are available. So our menu represents a typically easy-to-prepare meal, using some dried and packaged products from the south.

Nova Scotia

DINNER FOR 6

Fish Chowder p.75
Nova Scotia Oat Cakes p.136
Cucumber Salad
Lemon Squares p.169

Nova Scotia has an interesting history. Despite its name — New Scotland — the Micmac Indians were there first, and the French were the first European settlers, although it is possible that Celtic monks from Iceland settled on Cape Breton Island some seven centuries earlier. Rumblings from the British started in the eighteenth century and many of the French Acadian settlers were forcibly removed from their land. The Lunenberg area was settled by German immigrants in the 1750s and a large Scottish contingent arrived in the early 1800s.

Although the Atlantic coast is stormy in winter, the slopes facing the Gulf of St. Lawrence and the Bay of Fundy are sheltered, and the land is fertile. The Annapolis Valley has long been famous for its beauty and its apples, and there are dairy, livestock and poultry farms in other parts of the province. The pulp and paper industry and fishing are also very important to the economy.

Our lunch menu shows some of the variety of Nova Scotia's history. Oatcakes are very Scottish, and are frequently served with a hearty fish chowder. Sour cream is a basic in German cooking, and makes a delicious salad with thinly sliced cucumbers.

Ontario

DINNER FOR 6

Ontario Cheddar Soup p.53
Apricot Chicken p.77
Piquant Peas p.121
Pot de Chocolat p.150

Ontario, as well as being Canada's most populous province, possesses the most varied terrain and climate in the country. Although for its latitude it ranks among the earth's coldest places, cacti nevertheless grow on Canada's southernmost tip: Point Pelee, Ontario. It is also known as the food basket of Canada, since just about every variety of livestock, fruit and vegetable can be grown or raised there. Strawberries are abundant in the south, while grapes, apricots and peaches are grown on the Niagara peninsula where there is also a flourishing wine industry.

Ontario is well known for its varieties of cheese, accounting for over 50% of Canada's cheese production. Their cheddar is most famous and it is shipped all over the world. Ontario is also Canada's largest producer of poultry, so it seems appropriate to include a delicious chicken recipe.

Prince Edward Island

DINNER FOR 6

Smoked Oyster Pâté p.43
Island Sole p.73
Sweet and Sour Salad p.63
P.E.I. Chocolate Cake p.171
or Bread Pudding p.146

Canada's smallest province has the mildest climate of all the Maritime provinces, and great natural beauty. The Micmac Indians called it "Abegweit", meaning "home cradled on the waves", and the French later named it Ile St. Jean. The British took over in 1758, and eventually named it Prince Edward Island, after Queen Victoria's father.

P.E.I. is probably best known for its high-quality potatoes, which grow well in the famous red soil, and which are shipped all over the world, including South America and North Africa. Potatoes play an important part in the daily diet of the islanders, appearing in both festive and everyday dishes, including our P.E.I. chocolate cake. More than fifty percent of the land is farmland, but the fishing industry is almost equally important — lobsters being much sought after and, more prosaically perhaps, cod. Dairy farming is also a significant source of revenue.

Quebec

DINNER FOR 6

Quebec, with its French inheritance, is fortunate in being able to draw on cooking traditions and history somewhat different from those in the rest of Canada.

The Quebecois tend to be passionate about their food, and there are more food and wine societies in Quebec than anywhere else in the country. There is a great variety of traditions in cooking: haute cuisine, in the classic French sense, and the home cooking of old Quebec, along with dishes which can be very English, very French, or strongly influenced by New England cooking.

Maple syrup is probably Quebec's best-known product. Methods of collecting it have not changed much since the Indians first discovered it centuries ago. The sap of sugar-maple trees is tapped (usually in March each year) and then boiled to remove the surplus water. The syrup which results is uniquely delicious and is used in several famous dessert recipes, of which our maple mousse is one. Early settlers used maple syrup to make maple beer, wine and vinegar.

Saskatchewan

DINNER FOR 6

Prairie Soup p.55
Roast Duck p.84
Wild Rice Casserole p.133
Saskatchewan Fruit Pie p.167

Saskatchewan's name comes from the Cree word "Kisiskatchewan", meaning "the river that flows swiftly", from which of course came the name of the town of Swift Current. Its winters can be fiercely cold, and summers are correspondingly hot and dry — an ideal climate for the great prairie grainfields.

Most people think of Saskatchewan as being Canada's breadbasket, since so much wheat is grown there, but its potash fields are the largest in the world and supply agriculture and industry.

Many Germans and Ukrainians immigrated to the province, and their heritage influences tastes in food, as does that of the native Indians and the Scandinavians.

The famous wild rice is in fact not a true rice, but a kind of wild grass which grows in shallow water in the marsh area of freshwater lakes and rivers. Its crunchy texture and nutlike flavour go particularly well with wild duck, a favourite of Saskatchewan hunters.

Caribbean

DINNER FOR 6

Callaloo – Trinidad p.51
Loma de Puerco – Panama p.87
Stuffed Christophene – Trinidad p.117
Haitian Rice – Haiti p.131
Daiquiri Soufflé – Puerto Rico p.163

A world of delight awaits you in the sunny Caribbean. Golden beaches and turquoise seas, swaying palms and warm breezes set the scene for the music and laughter that come so naturally to the island people. Visitors are treated to the infectious rhythm of the calypso and the steel bands, and partying is a way of life.

Along with all the conviviality go good food and drinks. Catering for a crowd means barbecueing over coals in great oil drums, or serving hops (huge crusty rolls) with ham or seasoned shark. Rum, of course, is the most popular alcoholic drink, and is used as a base for many exotic drinks such as rum punch, pina colada, or just plain rum and coke.

Fish is plentiful in the Islands, with everything from tiny half-pound flying fish to great tuna or marlin weighing 100 pounds or more. Goat meat is common in Jamaica, and suckling pig is often roasted for festive occasions. Tropical fruits grow in great abundance throughout the islands. Any backyard could have mango, pawpaw and citrus trees, along with bananas, avocadoes and guavas.

China

DINNER FOR 6

Fried Wontons p.48
Plum Sauce p.138
Wonton Soup p.58
Ginger Braised Chicken p.79
Barbecued Pork p.87
Fried Rice p.130
Oriental Custard p.156

China is a land of many contrasts. The climate varies from the steamy tropics in the South to the snows of the Himalayas and the barren wastes of the Gobi Desert. Languages and dialects are many and varied, and so it is with the cuisine.

Chinese cooking falls into three main categories. In Northern China the food is strongly flavoured, using dark soy sauce, bean paste and garlic. The second area is along the Yangtze River basin, where probably the most sophisticated cuisine is to be found. Food is often steamed and spices are widely used. From the South comes the style of cooking with which North Americans are most familiar — stir-fried vegetables, still crisp and crunchy, succulent chicken and light soy sauce.

A family meal in China is a shared experience. Each person will have their own bowl of rice, but will use their chopsticks to help themselves from the centrally placed dishes of meat, fish and vegetables. Soup is frequently served, and bird's nest soup is one of the most interesting. The nests are gathered near the sea, as vitamin- rich sea moss will have been used by the birds to make the nests. They are carefully washed and cleaned before using!

No Chinese meal is complete without the ritual cups of fragrant tea.

East Germany

DINNER FOR 4

Spreewald Style Fish p.73
Dilled Potatoes
Apricot Flan p.164

At 50,000 square miles, East Germany is about half the size of neighbouring West Germany, and as can be expected from a once unified area, the cuisine of the two countries is very similar. Subtle differences are due to influences from countries on its eastern border, Poland and Czechoslovakia, as evidenced by liberal use of seasonings such as paprika, caraway, dill and vinegar. Meat is often pickled, as in the famous Sauerbraten, and sausages come in an endless variety. Although chicken and turkey are increasing in popularity, goose and pork are still the most common choices for entrées, especially for festive occasions. Fish and seafood are also popular, and our Spreewald style fish is a lovely company dish.

Many German dishes and food items have been adopted enthusiastically by North Americans. The ones that immediately spring to mind are hamburgers, hot dogs, rye bread and pumpernickel; but some lesser known but equally popular food items are the jelly doughnut, originating as the "Berliner Pfankuchen" and Boston Cream Pie, known originally in Germany as "Moor's Head".

Finland

DINNER FOR 6

Karelian Stew p.95
Rutabaga Casserole p.124
Cloudberry Parfait p.151

The eating habits of the Finns reflect the ruggedness and northerly climate of their country. After all, summer in Finland lasts only for about two months, which makes for an extremely short growing season.

Finnish food also shows the influence of Sweden and Russia — Finland's version of the smorgasbord, for example, is called Voileipapoyta. Breads and cooked grains are staples in the Finnish diet, along with meat, potatoes and dairy products. The country is famous for its cheeses, and fruits in season are prized. Berries are often preserved — although Finns are not noted for being particularly sweet-toothed.

Two Finnish liquors are Hakka (made from cloudberries) and Mesi Marjo (made from the arctic brambleberry). It has been said of the Finns that once a bottle is open, it is almost a point of honour with them not to leave anything in it.

France

DINNER FOR 4

Roquefort Tarts p.41
Paupiettes Lyonnaises p.105
Chocolat à l'Orange p.149
or Glace au Citron p.153

French cuisine is, of course, legendary; the most praised and emulated in the civilized world. For centuries French chefs have developed wonderful regional dishes that have become favourites on restaurant menus the world over. Most recently, the French have led the way towards today's lighter style of eating. "Cuisine minceur" for the diet conscious, has taken over in popularity from the rich sauces for which France is so famous. The secret of French cooking lies in the expert use of seasonings. Herbs and sauces turn the simplest of ingredients into dishes fit for a king.

It is difficult to think of any area of cooking in which the French do not excel, and for which there are not French terms and expressions. Hors d'oeuvres, pâtés and entrées are followed by wonderful French cheeses such as Brie and Camembert, and by desserts and pastries, soufflés and éclairs.

The wines, brandies and liqueurs of France proved a true complement to any French meal.

Great Britain

DINNER FOR 6

Parsnip Soup p.53
English Pot Roast p.93
Baked Potatoes
English Trifle p.154

Much vile calumny has been written about British cooking. True, the national propensity to overcook cabbage is legendary, as are pots of tea brewed so strong as to make the toes curl. But no one who has ever tasted such wonders as fresh baked scones spread with clotted cream and thick strawberry jam, or real Dover sole accompanied by tiny new potatoes, or any of the marvellous cheeses — notably Cheddar, Cheshire, and Stilton — can complain that British food is dull.

Roasting meat on a spit was the preferred method centuries ago, because the British liked their meat strongly flavoured. Even today the size of the roast, or "joint" as it is called, is reduced by roasting and the flavour concentrated. The popular slow-cooked pot roast also originated long ago when peat was commonly used as a fuel. The peat fire could not be made hot enough for spit roasting, so the meat was covered and cooked long and slowly.

Trifle varies with the cook who is making it, and it is hard to describe. Some cooks have a heavy hand with the sherry, some use no sherry at all, but when all is said and done there can be something quite regal about a trifle.

Greece

DINNER FOR 6

Spanokopita p.49
Roast Lamb with Potatoes p.102
Zatziki p.117
Kourabiedes p.178

Greek cuisine is centuries old. It was the first European country to develop a particular style of cooking, by blending and combining spices and ingredients to produce unique and delightful flavours. Honey, lemon and cinnamon are flavourings frequently used in Greek cooking. In the civilization of ancient Greece, foods were thought to have special powers: honey was eaten before athletes entered the arena, and according to Greek mythology garlic was thought to ward off evil spirits and to cleanse the blood. Feta cheese, especially popular in North America today as an essential ingredient in Greek salads, was once considered to be an aphrodisiac.

Phyllo, or Fillo means "leaf" in Greek, and this paper thin pastry is used to wrap both sweet and savoury fillings to create such delicacies as spanokopita and baklava. Richly seasoned lamb is commonly served throughout Greece, frequently with a cooling cucumber and yogurt salad. And what better way to end a meal than with Kourabiedes, the most popular of Greek cookies. Always baked in crescent shapes, they are served on every special occasion.

Hungary
DINNER FOR 6

Sour Cream Lettuce Salad p.64
Chicken Paprika p.78
Dumplings p.129
Dilled Zucchini p.125
Brandied Pears p.157

Hungary is a small land-locked country in central Europe, with a climate of short, hot summers and cold winters. The mighty Danube divides the country, as it flows on its way to Romania and the Black Sea in the South East, and acts as an important international waterway for Hungarian trade. Major exports are machinery, textiles, wine made from Tokay grapes, and the famed Hungarian paprika.

Paprika is used profusely in Hungary, and many families in the countryside still grow their own and hang it on strings from the eaves of their houses to dry. Our menu, of course, has a paprika dish, as well as liberal amounts of that other Hungarian staple, sour cream. Another world-famous dish is Hungarian goulash, and the Magyar people also love thick, hearty soups, spicy sausages, caviar, and wonderful pastries and strudels.

Hungarians are very hospitable people, and guests are plied with good food and wine before the singing and dancing begin. Hungary has a rich tradition of folklore and music, of rhythmic, foot-stomping dancing and of beautiful national costumes.

Italy

DINNER FOR 6

From the land of gondoliers and hot political passion comes an astonishing diversity of foods and wines. The Greeks gave Italy the name "Oenotria", meaning Land of Vines, because vines grow just about everywhere. In fact Italy is the largest wine producer in the world, and wine is an everyday drink to Italians.

It is said that pasta originated in China (the northern Chinese use wheat in making their noodles) and was brought back to Italy in dried form by Marco Polo. Tomatoes may also have been introduced to Italy from China. Pasta is widely used, of course, but contrary to some popular North American opinion it is not the dietary mainstay of all Italians. Rice, "riso", which grows on the plain of the River Po in northern Italy, is much used, and risotto is the method of cooking it.

Veal is something of a luxury these days, as it is almost everywhere, but Italian veal is famous: "vitello" is a calf two to three months old, and "vitellone" is more or less a teenager — neither calf nor adult.

Cheese and fruit are a must at every meal, and the country is rich in marvellous cheeses: consider Gorgonzola, Parmesan, and Mozzarella, to give only a few examples. For dessert, Italians are famed for their "gelati" or ice-cream, in all its wonderful varieties.

India

DINNER FOR 8

Lamb Curry p.104
Cucumber Raita p.116
Rice with Peas p.129
Dhal p.134
Chapattis p.134
Carrot Halva p.149

Food customs in India are limited to a certain extent by Hindu and Muslim dietary laws. Devout Hindus, for example, eat no meat at all, and Muslims will not eat pork. The kitchen and the preparation of food are regarded as somewhat sacred, and it is customary to remove one's shoes before entering the kitchen, since the shoes may be made from animal hide.

Indian cooking includes the use of many different kinds of spices, combinations of which vary from family to family and place to place. All areas of the subcontinent depend on cereals and legumes, and pulses (the edible seeds of various leguminous crops) are eaten generally at least once a day, often in a sauce called "dhal". Vegetables and fruits are mostly eaten in the form of chutneys and relishes. Raita is a cool, refreshing salad often served as a relish with curried meats.

The highly seasoned foods characteristic of Indian cooking often are followed by desserts that soothe the tongue as well as being tasty, such as carrot halva.

Japan

DINNER FOR 6

Chirashi Sushi p.59
Yakitori p.77
Sukiyaki p.97
Goma Ae p.115
Mandarin Snow Sponge p.155

Japanese cuisine is becoming popular in North America, and for good reason. Its simplicity and artistry are in marked contrast to much of the fussiness which sometimes passes for haute cuisine in the West. A lot can be learned by taking heed of the way the Japanese show Shinto and Buddhist influence, as seen in the harmonious arrangement of food and garnish on the plate.

Rice is the staple grain, usually eaten by itself between dishes, or at the end of the meal, although noodles are also popular. Japanese salads, unlike ours, consist of lightly-cooked vegetables and rice, or noodles, chilled and served in a vinegar dressing.

Sukiyaki (suki meaning hoe, yaki meaning cook) is derived from Japan's early history when the peasants were not allowed to eat meat. So they developed a method of cooking, quickly and on the spot, whatever game they could find. Hence today sukiyaki is always cooked at the table. Yakitori is chicken, usually marinated, cooked on a skewer or spit over an open grill.

Tea is without doubt the most important beverage in Japan, and the gracious tea ceremony is typical of Japanese courtesy and charm.

Middle East

DINNER FOR 4

Middle Eastern Salad – Jordan p.64
Mansaf – Jordan p.103
Turkish Vegetable Mélange – Turkey p.113
Apple Nut Pudding – Turkey p.145
or Date and Banana Dessert – Jordan p.145

There is an old Arabic proverb that says "today is better than tomorrow", and perhaps that is why the Arabic people take such pleasure in mealtime rituals. Feasts are prepared and guests invited to celebrate any occasion. Meals are usually eaten with the hands, and afterwards friends linger together over bowls of fruit and small cups of thick, sweet coffee. The largest dish in the world, according to the Guinness Book of Records, is served at Bedouin wedding feasts. Cooked eggs are stuffed into fish, the fish into cooked chickens, chickens into sheep, and the sheep into a camel which is roasted over a huge fire.

Bulgur, which is wheat that has been boiled and dried, is probably the forerunner of bread as it dates from ancient times. It is used in the Middle East in soups and stuffings and as a substitute for rice. Yogurt is another popular food, and is said to fortify the soul.

Sheep are the most common source of meat in the Middle East, and our Mansaf (or big meal) uses lamb, almonds and other traditional seasonings. The dish can easily be expanded to serve a crowd of guests, and in Jordan would be supplemented with stuffed vine leaves, rolled up pancakes, stuffed peppers and tomatoes, to make a magnificent buffet style meal.

New Zealand

DINNER FOR 6

Oyster Bisque p.54
Roast Stuffed Leg of Lamb p.101
Buttered Carrots and Broccoli
Fruit Meringue p.161

It is said that sheep in New Zealand outnumber people by twenty to one, and indeed New Zealand lamb is world-renowned. Careful distinctions are made as to the age of the animal: spring lamb is the youngest and most tender, hogget is lamb butchered at between nine and twenty months, and anything older than that becomes mutton.

Less well known is the excellence of the local seafood — oysters and lobsters being particularly good — and New Zealanders are also fond of dairy products. Their consumption of butter, milk and ice-cream is prodigious. Kiwi fruit (also known as Chinese gooseberry) is native to the country. It, and other fruits and vegetables, are grown mainly on the North Island, where the climate ranges from temperate to sub-tropical.

Many of the eating habits of the British have been transplanted to New Zealand: they are some of the world's greatest tea drinkers, and although there is a local wine industry, beer remains the most favoured beverage.

Republic of Ireland

DINNER FOR 8

Potato and Herb Soup p.57
Glazed Cornish Game Hens p.85
Irish Autumn Pudding p.147
or Irish Bananas p.146

Generally speaking, Irish cooking tends to be quite simple. Oatmeal is traditional, although potatoes were adopted as a staple food by the peasants in the eighteenth century because most of the other crops they grew, (such as oats, wheat and barley), for their largely absentee Scottish and English landlords, were exported. Potatoes, though, were originally brought to Ireland by the English, and are used today in a myriad of ways: they can be put into cakes and breads, boiled with or without jackets, fried, mashed, baked, or combined with other foods. They are always used in the popular everyday dish of Irish stew.

Nearly one-third of the working population of Ireland is employed in agriculture, and the Irish use dairy products frequently in their cooking. For instance, their famous soda bread uses buttermilk.

Irish stout is a favourite beverage, and Irish whiskey is very popular. The well-known Irish coffee does not, as the saying goes, have very deep emerald roots; it was invented only a few decades ago in order to improve whiskey sales.

South Korea

DINNER FOR 6

Sour and Hot Soup p.54
Bul-Ko-Kee p.96
Gut Kuri Kimchi p.118
Fresh Fruit

South Korea is a country of rugged mountains and valleys, with a temperate and humid climate. The people are very hospitable, and the giving of gifts and the sharing of meals with guests is an integral part of life. As in Japan, Koreans remove their shoes to eat, and sit on cushions at low tables. However, the food and the seasonings used are very different. Meals follow a typical pattern of soup, fish or meat, kimchi, rice, and fresh fruit. Tea is not as popular as in other Oriental countries, and instead barley water or ginseng are served.

Koreans grow more vegetables than other people in the Orient. Kimchi is almost a national obsession and is served at every meal. It is a highly seasoned pickled cabbage, often made with the addition of turnip, cucumber and other vegetables. It is stored underground in huge jars the size of a man, and is left to ferment for at least a month. Frequently, communal backyards are used for the sole purpose of storing kimchi.

Bul-Ko-Kee is another universally popular dish. Spicy strips of beef are broiled or barbecued to perfection.

Spain
DINNER FOR 8

Gazpacho p.52
Paella p.81
Chestnut Soufflé p.161

In the town of Jerez de la Fontera in Southern Spain are little bars where tapas, delicious morsels of food, become a banquet. Spanish olives and cheeses, ham, lobster claws and miniature steaks, are served with a copita of the world famous wine to which Jerez has given its name — sherry. The English discovered sherry and it has become one of the world's most popular drinks to serve with appetizers.

The warm Mediterranean sun provides an ideal climate for production of fruits and vegetables, which are a major source of export for Spain. Tomatoes and green peppers form the base for gazpacho, the chilled soup indigenous to Spain where each city takes pride in its own variety. And no good cook's kitchen is complete without a bottle of Spanish olive oil!

Fishing is an important industry in Spain, sardines and anchovies being export specialties. The pride of the Costa Brava is paella, that wonderful meal-in-a-dish of rice, chicken and shellfish, seasoned with saffron and piqued with tomatoes and garlic — a dish to be enjoyed the world over.

Sweden

DINNER FOR 12

Herring and Beet Salad p.62
Swedish Glazed Ham p.92
Jansson's Temptation p.123
Sweet and Sour Red Cabbage p.118
Swedish Spritz Cookies p.176

Sweden is the largest of the Scandinavian countries, on the same latitude as Denmark in the South, and stretching way up into the Arctic Circle, the Land of the Midnight Sun. It is a highly industrialized country, and a leader in social reform, enjoying one of the highest standards of living in the world.

The Scandinavian smorgasbord has been adopted by foreigners as an extravagant buffet, with many delicacies heaped onto the dinner plate at one time. In Scandinavia, however, the smorgasbord is a meal of many taste surprises, with the individual dishes served in small portions as separate courses.

Herring is without doubt the most important item on the menu, and a festive meal always commences with a herring dish and the traditional glass of aquavit. Other fish dishes may follow, and then could come cold cuts, liver pâté, egg concoctions, and meat balls. The main meat dish will be accompanied by vegetables. Salad, cheese, a light dessert and strong coffee will round out the fare. A meal of such gastronomic proportions will take all evening to consume, accompanied by much singing and laughter.

Switzerland

DINNER FOR 6

Cheese Fondue p.108
Salad
Mandel Torte p.172

It is easy to gain a great deal of weight on a visit to Switzerland. The bread is wonderful, and so are the pastries, the chocolate, and the cream. There is also an irresistible way of cooking potatoes called "roesti" (boiled, diced and fried, using Swiss cheese and onion).

Although their country is home to a number of renowned hotel and cooking schools, the Swiss themselves tend to have simpler tastes in food. Bread and cheese are probably most used, since meat and fish are expensive. Cheese fondue is perhaps the best-known dish outside the country; it is most popular among French-speaking Swiss, and involves Gruyère and Emmenthal cheese, white wine and a dash of Kirsch. It is a pleasant custom to pause half-way through the meal to have a small glass of Kirsch to help the digestion, and anyone whose chunk of bread falls off their fork into the cheese mixture is required to pay the penalty of buying a bottle of wine. Swiss wine can be very good indeed, although for various reasons little of it is exported. White wines are made predominantly with Fendant grapes, which produce dry, slightly sparkling wines, and there are vineyards in just about every district.

We have chosen to round off our menu with Mandel Torte, a special occasion almond pastry that looks as good as it tastes.

Thailand

DINNER FOR 8

Lemon Prawn Soup p.56
Thai Chicken Curry p.82
Sweet Fried and Crisp Noodles p.126
Steamed Rice
Coconut Ice Cream with Lichees
or Rambatan Fruit

The people of Thailand have taken the culinary traditions of their neighbours, India and China, and made them uniquely their own. A third century Chinese poem suggested that food should have five characteristics - bitter, salt, sour, hot and sweet - and Thai food reflects this.

There are vast rice fields in the central plains of Thailand, with livestock and varied agriculture in the higher plateaus. Seafood is abundant in the Strait of Malacca, and a great deal of fish is eaten. There is a Buddhist teaching cautioning against the killing of live creatures, but the Thai people rationalize this by not killing fish, but rather setting traps so the fish enter them and die.

A Thai invitation to a meal will be to "Kin Kao" or "eat rice", and the table will be set with assorted dishes of curry, soups, salads and vegetables around a central dish of plain, boiled rice. Guests will be given a large dinner plate, to serve themselves from the central dishes, and will use a spoon and fork to eat. A soup bowl and spoon will be on one side, and a beer or wine glass on the other. The table will be beautifully decorated. Flowers will be scattered on the table, and carved vegetables will garnish the dishes.

Thai people love the peppery heat of chilies, and it is said that when a bald-headed man feels a slight dampness on his head, then the chili is just right!

Tonga

DINNER FOR 6

Ota Ika p.60
Lu Pulu p.96
Pele Sipi p.102
Ufi Haka p.124
Tropical Fruit Salad p.159

Tonga comprises a chain of 150 small, friendly islands, and is the only surviving independent kingdom in the South Pacific. A British protectorate since 1900, it was ruled for nearly 50 years by gracious Queen Salote, who was succeeded by her son. Tongans are tall and strong, and proud of their high rate of literacy. Primary education is compulsory and most Tongans are landowners with one of the highest standards of living in Polynesia.

The food of Tonga, as with the other Polynesian islands, is typically quite bland. Mild curry and salt are the favourite seasonings, and the meat and cream from the ubiquitous coconut are frequently used. The traditional method of cooking in Tonga is by wrapping the prepared food in large leaves and baking in the úmu, a pit which is used as an underground oven. Preparation of the úmu is time consuming, however, so food for everyday cooking is known as "haka", which is simply boiling in water and coconut cream over an open fire. Tongans enjoy barbecueing, and a typical feast will include suckling pig, raw, marinated fish, a yam dish and barbecued octopus.

Breadfruit is a staple food in the South Pacific, and was brought from Polynesia to the Caribbean to supplement the West Indian diet. H.M.S. Bounty was loaded with breadfruit trees bound for Jamaica when the famous mutiny occurred in 1789.

Union of Soviet Socialist Republics

DINNER FOR 6

Fish and Mushroom Roll p.71
Salad
Rhubarb Kissel p.158

If we believed everything the movies used to tell us, we would be convinced that all Russians eat nothing but heavy rye bread, cabbage and potatoes, washed down either with gallons of vodka or tea while stamping snow off their boots. As with all clichés, there is a certain amount of truth to it, but when we consider the different traditions of the Caucasus, Georgia, Armenia and the Baltic and Central Asian regions we realize how limited it is.

The Caucasus, for instance, is much influenced by Eastern Mediterranean cooking. Eggplant purée is a famous appetizer — sometimes called poor man's caviar — and salads (not usually the green, leafy kind) are eaten often. Georgians use walnuts in many ways: as oil, for example, or as a paste. Zakuski, a sort of smorgasbord of hors d'oeuvres including smoked fish or salt herring, boiled potatoes and pickled vegetables, shows a Scandinavian influence. Armenian cooking tends to follow the Turkish style.

If the Soviet Union can be said to have a national dessert, it would be Kissel, a puréed fruit concoction, usually made from one of the more tart fruits. It can be made thick enough to set, or thin enough to pour.

United States of America

DINNER FOR 8

Roast Turkey p.83
Cornbread Stuffing p.136
Cranberry–Orange Relish p.137
Broccoli Casserole p.114
Potatoes and Yeast Rolls
Chiffon Pumpkin Pie Supreme p.166

Visitors to the United States could be forgiven for believing that the American national dish consists of hamburger and french fries, that cola is the national beverage, and snacking the national pastime. In fact, American eating habits are as diverse as its geography and the immigrants who came to settle there.

The earliest pioneers learned from the Indians how to prepare various dishes made from corn, and pumpkin was native to North America long before any white settlers arrived. It was used for animal feed, as well as in making a kind of molasses.

As in every country, American comedians use traditional foods as a target. It has been said that "a cranberry is a cherry with an acid condition", and "broccoli is something that's difficult to say anything nice about except that it has no bones". Our menu, however, is the traditional Thanksgiving turkey dinner, and comedians notwithstanding, includes delicious ways of using both broccoli and cranberries.

West Germany

DINNER FOR 6

West German Pork p.88
Red Cabbage and New Potatoes
West German Cheesecake p.170

The regions of West Germany vary widely, with noticeable differences being detected in their architecture, dialects and customs, as well as in their cuisine. Although sausages, pork and cabbage are certainly representative of West German cooking, they are by no means the only specialties. Potatoes were introduced to Germany in the 1700's, and have now eclipsed dumplings and noodles as a popular entrée accompaniment. "Kartoffelpuffer" or potato pancakes, appear often, either as a vegetable side dish, or slightly sweetened and served with applesauce as a dessert. Game dishes are also abundant, along with such dishes as snails and quiche introduced from neighbouring France and Switzerland. A rich dessert is a common ending to a meal, and our cheesecake is an interesting variation on an old favourite.

"Prosit", the national toast, is heard from mid-morning to midnight, in fine restaurants, street-side snack bars, and homes. It is an integral part of every meal, and can take the form of a large stein of domestic beer, a glass of wine made from grapes grown along the Rhine, or a quickly-downed shot of never-to-be-forgotten schnapps.

Starters

Roquefort Tarts
FRANCE

Makes 8

Somewhat like a quiche, these rich appetizers may be served on a bed of lettuce seasoned with vinaigrette dressing, or made into smaller tarts to serve with cocktails.

Pastry:

¼ cup	*butter*	*50 ml*
1 tbsp	*sugar*	*15 ml*
⅔ cup	*flour plus 1 tbsp*	*190 ml*
⅛ tsp	*salt*	*pinch*
1	*egg*	*1*

Mix above ingredients together using a fork, wooden spoon or food processor until a moist ball of dough is formed. Grease eight 3 in/8 cm tart pans with butter. Divide dough into equal parts and without rolling, line tart pans by pressing dough into shape with your fingers. Set aside.

Preheat oven to 375°F/190°C.

Filling:

¼ lb	*Roquefort or Danish Blue cheese*	*125 g*
1	*large egg*	*1*
½ cup	*light cream*	*125 ml*
⅛ tsp	*pepper*	*pinch*

Crumble cheese evenly over tart shells. In a small bowl combine egg, cream and pepper, then pour into cheese-filled tarts. Bake for 30 minutes and allow to sit for 5 minutes before serving.

Liptauer Cheese
AUSTRIA

Makes about 2 cups/500 ml

Thinly sliced rye or pumpernickel bread should accompany this easy-to-make spread.

1 cup	*cream-style cottage cheese*	*250 ml*
½ cup	*unsalted butter, softened*	*125 ml*
1 tbsp	*Hungarian paprika*	*15 ml*
⅛ tsp	*black pepper, freshly ground*	*pinch*
¼ tsp	*salt*	*1 ml*
1 tsp	*caraway seeds*	*5 ml*
1 tsp	*dry mustard*	*5 ml*
1 tsp	*capers, finely chopped*	*5 ml*
1 tbsp	*chives, finely chopped*	*15 ml*
½ cup	*sour cream (or less)*	*125 ml*

Garnish:

anchovy fillets
parsley sprigs
chives, finely chopped
radishes, finely chopped

With a wooden spoon, press the cottage cheese through a sieve into a mixing bowl.

In a large bowl, cream butter and beat in cheese, paprika, black pepper, salt, caraway seeds, mustard, capers, chives and sour cream. Continue beating vigorously with a wooden spoon or electric mixer until mixture forms a smooth paste. Mound into serving dish and refrigerate for 2 hours.

To garnish, decorate spread with rolled anchovy fillets inserted with wooden tooth picks, a sprinkling of paprika and a few sprigs of parsley.

To serve, spread mixture on bread and set out chives and radishes to sprinkle on top.

Armstrong Cheddar Cheese Balls
BRITISH COLUMBIA

Makes 42

Keep these tangy make-ahead appetizers ready in your freezer.

2 cups	*medium cheddar cheese, grated*	*500 ml*
½ cup	*unsalted butter*	*125 ml*
1 cup	*flour*	*250 ml*
1 tsp	*paprika*	*5 ml*
1	*8 oz jar pimento-stuffed green olives*	*250 ml*

Mix cheese, butter, flour and paprika using a fork or food processor until dough forms a moist ball. Drain olives, rinse thoroughly in cold water and pat dry. Using a lightly floured board and rolling pin, roll dough out to approximately ¼ in/6 mm. Cut small rounds with a 2 in/5 cm cookie cutter. Place olive in centre and mould dough around olive to form a smooth ball. Freeze for at least 24 hours.

Cook frozen on a cookie sheet in a 400°F/205°C oven for 15 minutes. Serve hot.

Smoked Oyster Pâte
PRINCE EDWARD ISLAND

Makes 1 cup/250 ml

So easy to make, and a favourite for all smoked oyster fans.

1	*4 oz package cream cheese, at room temperature*	*125 g*
1	*3 ⅝ oz tin smoked oysters, chopped*	*104 g*
1 tbsp	*mayonnaise*	*15 ml*
1 tbsp	*sherry, brandy, or milk*	*15 ml*
1 tsp	*onion juice*	*5 ml*
	pepper	
	parsley	

Blend all ingredients except parsley. Spoon pâté into a serving dish, cover with plastic wrap and refrigerate at least 4 hours.

Garnish with sprig of parsley and serve with a variety of crackers.

Cretons à la Maison
QUEBEC

Serves 6 to 8

Serve this appetizer as you would pâté, with crackers or french bread.

1 lb	*minced pork fat, with rind*	*500 g*
2 lbs	*minced pork*	*1 kg*
1 cup	*boiling water*	*250 ml*
½ cup	*onions, diced*	*125 ml*
2 tsp	*salt*	*10 ml*
¼ tsp	*pepper*	*1 ml*
¼ tsp	*ground cloves*	*1 ml*
¼ tsp	*ground nutmeg*	*1 ml*
1 tbsp	*white wine*	*15 ml*
	preserved crabapple	
	sprig of fresh parsley	

Render pork fat over low heat until golden brown, stirring frequently. Drain through cheesecloth, saving both rendered fat and cracklings. Pat cracklings with paper towel to remove excess fat. Combine minced pork and water. Simmer for about 1 hour, stirring occasionally to prevent sticking. Add remaining ingredients including cracklings. Cover and simmer for about 2 hours, stirring occasionally. Cool and mix well. If mixture looks particularly fatty remove approximately 1 tbsp/15 ml fat. Pour into a small loaf pan or mold which has been rinsed in cold water. Chill until firm, approximately 4 hours.

Garnish with preserved crabapple and sprig of parsley.

Clams in White Wine
ITALY

Serves 6

A must for all clam fans.

5 lbs	*fresh clams*	*2.5 kg*
	seawater or ¾ cup/75 ml salt per gallon/ 4 l water	
	rolled oats, a handful	
¼ cup	*olive oil*	*50 ml*
2	*cloves garlic, crushed*	*2*
½ cup	*fresh parsley, chopped*	*125 ml*
¾ cup	*dry white wine*	*200 ml*
⅛ tsp	*salt*	*pinch*
1	*loaf Italian bread, cut in chunks*	*1*

Put fresh clams into a bucket of sea water with a handful of rolled oats. Soak for 2 hours. Be sure to use 3 times as much water as clams.

Transfer clams into fresh seawater and soak a further 2 hours.

Scrub clams thoroughly and rinse in fresh water. Drain.

Heat oil in skillet to 400°F/200°C, add garlic and cook for 2 minutes.

Lower heat to 300°F/150°C, add clams and parsley. Cover and simmer for 5 minutes. Add wine and salt. Simmer, uncovered, for 10 minutes or until clams open.

Serve hot, in their shells, with chunks of bread. Spoon the extra sauce over the clams.

Seafood in Garlic Cream Sauce
AUSTRALIA

Serves 6

A marvellous way to begin a special dinner.

1 cup	*rice*	*250 ml*
⅓ cup	*butter*	*75 ml*
4	*cloves garlic, crushed*	*4*
1 lb	*large prawns or shrimps, shelled*	*500 g*
½ lb	*scallops, cut into bite-sized pieces*	*250 g*
½ cup	*whipping cream*	*125 ml*
¼ tsp	*salt*	*1 ml*
⅛ tsp	*pepper*	*pinch*
	chopped parsley or cayenne pepper to garnish	

Cook rice in boiling, salted water for 13 minutes or until just tender. Keep warm.

In frying pan melt butter, Sauté crushed garlic for 2 minutes, add seafood and cook for 2 to 3 minutes more. Remove seafood from pan using a slotted spoon, leaving juices. Keep seafood warm.

Add cream to juices and bring to a frothing boil. Cook for several minutes until cream becomes a thick sauce. Add salt and pepper to taste.

To serve, place rice in 6 individual serving dishes; add seafood, cover with sauce and garnish with chopped parsley or cayenne pepper.

Pacific Shrimp Sauté
BRITISH COLUMBIA

Serves 8

Shrimp in garlic-wine sauce - guests will love it!

¼ cup	*butter*	*50 ml*
2	*cloves garlic, crushed*	*2*
1 lb	*fresh shrimp, cooked and shelled*	*500 g*
1 cup	*dry white wine*	*250 ml*
¼ cup	*fresh parsley, chopped*	*50 ml*
	crackers or French bread	

In medium skillet, melt butter. Add garlic and shrimp, cook 5 minutes, stirring occasionally. Add wine and parsley. Cook for 3 minutes. Transfer to a chafing dish and keep warm.

Serve from chafing dish, using toothpicks and accompanied by a choice of crackers or french bread.

Prawn Kokoda

FIJI

Serves 6

Raw prawns "cooked" overnight in lime juice and coconut milk make a delightful seafood cocktail. Serve with your favourite crackers or melba toast.

1 lb	*fresh, raw prawns*	*500 g*
2	*cloves garlic, crushed*	2
½ tsp	*salt*	*2 ml*
⅛ tsp	*pepper*	*pinch*
4	*juice of 4 limes*	4
1 cup	*coconut milk or cream*	*250 ml*

Garnish:

1 cup	*celery leaves, finely chopped*	*250 ml*
1	*green pepper, finely diced*	1
¾ cup	*green onions, sliced*	*200 ml*
	lettuce, shredded	
1	*tomato, thinly sliced*	1

Clean, peel and chop prawns. Place in a bowl with crushed garlic, salt and pepper. Add lime juice, then coconut cream and stir well. Cover and refrigerate for 12 hours.

Before serving, add celery leaves, green pepper and onion. Toss gently and serve on a bed of shredded lettuce and garnish with tomato slices.

Fried Wontons

CHINA

Makes 72

Serve as a crispy appetizer with a plum sauce dip.

¼ lb	*shrimp meat, finely chopped*	*250 g*
2	*green onions, finely chopped*	2
½ in	*piece ginger root, peeled and grated*	*1.3 cm*
6	*canned water chestnuts, drained and chopped*	6
2 tbsp	*parsley, chopped*	*30 ml*
1 tbsp	*soy sauce*	*15 ml*
1	*clove garlic, crushed*	1
2 tsp	*sesame oil*	*10 ml*
2 tsp	*cornstarch*	*10 ml*
¼ tsp	*salt*	*1 ml*
72	*3 in/7.5 cm wonton wrappers*	72
	oil for deep frying	

Combine shrimp meat and following nine ingredients. Place ½ tsp/2 ml mixture on each wonton wrapper. Brush edges with water. Fold in half to form a triangle, pinching edges to seal. Bring 2 points from ends of folded side together, overlapping and moistening so they will seal.

Cover wontons and refrigerate until serving time.

Heat oil in deep fryer to 360°F/180°C (not too hot, or filling will not cook). Deep fry about 6 wontons at a time for 2 to 3 minutes until golden. Remove with slotted spoon and drain on paper towels.

Serve immediately.

Note: If making wonton soup, reserve 24 uncooked wontons.

Spanokopita
GREECE

Serves 8

Spanokopita, a spinach pie in light, crunchy phyllo pastry, is a favourite dish in Greece when friends gather to eat and chat.

2 lbs	*fresh spinach*	*1 kg*
1	*onion, chopped*	*1*
¼ cup	*butter*	*50 ml*
1 cup	*cream*	*250 ml*
5	*eggs*	*5*
1 cup	*feta cheese, finely crumbled*	*250 ml*
½ tsp	*salt*	*2 ml*
¼ tsp	*pepper*	*1 ml*
⅛ tsp	*nutmeg*	*pinch*
½ cup	*butter, melted*	*125 ml*
½ lb	*phyllo pastry*	*250 g*

Wash and dry spinach. Tear into bite-sized pieces. Sauté onion in butter until golden brown. Add spinach and sauté a few minutes longer. Set aside to cool.

Preheat oven to 350°F/180°C.

In a large bowl combine cream, eggs, cheese and spices. Add spinach and onion mixture; stir to blend.

Brush an 11 x 14 in/28 x 36 cm baking dish with melted butter. Layer half the phyllo pastry, one sheet at a time, in the pan, brushing each sheet with melted butter. Fold in the edges to fit the dish, if necessary. Add spinach mixture and layer remaining phyllo sheets, continuing to spread each with butter. Brush top sheet with butter. Score top layers into eight squares with the tip of a sharp knife (for easier cutting later).

Bake for 35 to 40 minutes, or until golden brown. Let sit for 10 minutes before serving.

Pumpkin Fritters
BOTSWANA

Makes 24

These delicious little snacks are traditionally made without salt, but for North American palates we have added just a touch.

1	*egg*	*1*
1 cup	*cold, cooked pumpkin, mashed*	*250 ml*
1 cup	*flour*	*250 ml*
1 tsp	*baking powder*	*5 ml*
1 tsp	*curry powder*	*5 ml*
1 tsp	*salt*	*5 ml*
	vegetable oil for deep frying	

Beat egg and add to pumpkin, flour, baking powder, curry and salt. Mix well. Using a small, deep saucepan, heat oil for frying and drop batter into the hot fat, 1 tsp/5 ml at a time. Fry for approximately 2 minutes at 325°F/165°C. Remove with slotted spoon and serve immediately.

Borscht
MANITOBA

Serves 6

Although borscht brings to mind beets, the word actually means any soup made with a variety of vegetables. Borscht improves if allowed to age in the refrigerator or freezer.

6	*medium beets, chopped*	*6*
2	*small onions, chopped*	*2*
2	*small carrots, chopped*	*2*
6 cups	*water*	*1.5 l*
2	*stalks celery with leaves, chopped*	*2*
1½ cups	*tomato juice*	*375 ml*
2 cups	*cabbage, finely chopped*	*500 ml*
2 tbsp	*fresh dill weed*	*30 ml*
1 tsp	*salt*	*5 ml*
¼ cup	*butter*	*50 ml*
1	*medium onion, sliced*	*1*
1 cup	*heavy cream*	*250 ml*

Chop beets, onions and carrots and combine with water in a large saucepan. Over medium heat, simmer soup, uncovered, for 45 minutes. Add celery and cook a further 30 minutes, stirring occasionally. Add tomato juice, cabbage, dill weed and salt. Simmer for 15 minutes. Melt butter in a small pan and sauté onion rings; add to soup pot. Add heavy cream and heat through. Serve immediately.
Note: If freezing borscht, omit heavy cream. Add cream after soup has been heated through.

Callaloo

TRINIDAD

Serves 6

A spicy soup, unique to the West Indies.

1 lb	*callaloo or spinach leaves*	*500 g*
7 cups	*chicken stock*	*1.6 l*
1	*onion, minced*	*1*
1	*clove garlic, crushed*	*1*
2	*green onions, chopped*	*2*
¼ tsp	*thyme*	*1 ml*
4 oz	*lean salt pork, cut in small cubes*	*125 g*
5 oz	*crabmeat*	*150 g*
¼ cup	*coconut milk*	*50 ml*
8 oz	*okras, fresh or frozen*	*250 g*
	salt	
	pepper	
	West Indian hot pepper sauce	

Chop callaloo or spinach and put in saucepan with stock, onion, garlic, green onions, thyme and salt pork. Cover and simmer for 40 minutes or until pork is soft.

Add crabmeat, coconut milk and okras, then cook for another 10 minutes. Season to taste with salt, pepper and hot pepper sauce.

Gazpacho
SPAIN

Serves 6

This tangy, tomato-based, chilled soup is a year-round favourite.

3	*medium tomatoes, finely chopped*	*3*
1	*medium cucumber, peeled, seeded and finely chopped*	*1*
1/3 cup	*onion, finely chopped*	*75 ml*
2 tbsp	*pimento, drained and chopped*	*30 ml*
1/2	*clove garlic, crushed*	*1/2*
2 tbsp	*olive oil*	*30 ml*
2 tbsp	*apple cider vinegar*	*30 ml*
1 tsp	*salt*	*5 ml*
1/4 tsp	*pepper*	*1 ml*
1/8 tsp	*cayenne pepper*	*pinch*
2/3 cup	*tomato juice*	*175 ml*
6	*ice cubes*	*6*
2 tbsp	*fresh parsley, chopped*	*30 ml*
4	*pitted black olives, sliced*	*4*

In a large bowl combine first five ingredients. Stir in oil, vinegar, salt, pepper and cayenne. Add tomato juice and blend well. Cover and refrigerate for several hours. Serve in soup bowls with an ice cube in the centre and a sprinkling of parsley and black olives.

Parsnip Soup
GREAT BRITAIN

Serves 6

Try this delicate cream soup with the sweet, nutty flavour of parsnips.

2 tbsp	*butter*	*30 ml*
1 1/2 lb	*parsnips, peeled and chopped*	*750 g*
1	*small onion, peeled and chopped*	*1*
3 cups	*chicken stock*	*750 ml*
1/2 tsp	*salt*	*2 ml*
1/8 tsp	*pepper*	*pinch*
1 1/4 cups	*light cream*	*300 ml*
2 tbsp	*fresh parsley, chopped*	*30 ml*

In a large saucepan, melt butter over medium heat. Add parsnips and onion and sauté for 5 minutes. Add stock, bring to the boil and simmer 15 minutes or until vegetables are soft. Purée in blender or food processor. Season and return purée to saucepan. Reheat gently, adding the desired amount of light cream.

To serve, decorate each bowl with chopped parsley.

Ontario Cheddar Soup

ONTARIO

Serves 6

A hearty, nourishing soup that is easy to make and easy on the pocket book.

3 tbsp	*butter or margarine*	*45 ml*
2	*large onions, minced*	*2*
2	*carrots, sliced*	*2*
1	*stalk celery, including leaves, sliced*	*1*
1	*parsnip, sliced (optional)*	*1*
1/4 cup	*flour*	*50 ml*
2 cups	*chicken bouillon*	*500 ml*
3 cups	*milk*	*750 ml*
3 cups	*medium cheddar cheese, grated*	*750 ml*

Sauté vegetables in butter for 10 minutes. Stir in flour and gradually add bouillon, stirring constantly to prevent lumps. Cook over medium heat for 15 minutes. Cool slightly before processing in a blender. Reheat and add milk. Stir constantly until thick, about 5 minutes. Reduce heat and simmer, uncovered, for 10 minutes. Do not boil. Stir in cheese and heat through until cheese melts.

Garnish with sprinkling of grated cheddar.

Oyster Bisque
NEW ZEALAND

Serves 6

This New Zealand specialty can be made a day ahead and reheated before serving.

1 tbsp	*butter*	*15 ml*
1 tbsp	*flour*	*15 ml*
2 cups	*milk*	*500 ml*
12	*fresh oysters, chopped in small pieces*	*12*
1/8 tsp	*mace*	*pinch*
1/2 tsp	*salt*	*2 ml*
1/8 tsp	*pepper*	*pinch*
1 cup	*light cream*	*250 ml*
2 tbsp	*fresh parsley, chopped*	*30 ml*

In a medium saucepan melt butter, stir in flour. Remove from heat and stir in milk plus any juice from oysters. Return to heat and cook for 2 minutes, stirring constantly. Add oysters to liquid along with mace, salt and pepper. Adjust seasonings.

If not using immediately, refrigerate. To serve, heat through, add light cream and heat through again. Garnish with chopped parsley.

Sour and Hot Soup
SOUTH KOREA

Serves 6 to 8

The distinctive spicy flavour of this soup is typical of Korean cuisine.

1 1/2 oz	*package dried black mushrooms*	*42.5 g*
2 oz	*can bamboo shoots*	*50 g*
2 oz	*ham*	*50 g*
6 cups	*chicken stock*	*1.5 l*
3 tbsp	*soy sauce*	*45 ml*
2 tbsp	*white vinegar*	*30 ml*
2 tbsp	*cornstarch*	*30 ml*
6 tbsp	*water*	*90 ml*
2	*eggs, beaten*	*2*
1 tsp	*white pepper*	*5 ml*
1/2 tsp	*salt*	*2 ml*

Soak mushrooms in water for 30 minutes. Drain well.
Shred mushrooms, bamboo shoots and ham.
Bring chicken stock to the boil, add mushrooms, bamboo shoots and ham. Cook for 3 minutes. Add soy sauce, vinegar, cornstarch (mixed with 6 tbsp/90 ml water), and cook for 2 more minutes or until soup is boiling.
Swirl beaten eggs into soup. Add pepper and salt, stir to blend and taste for seasoning. Serve immediately.

Prairie Soup

SASKATCHEWAN

Serves 6

A delightful soup for a special autumn dinner.

1/4 cup	*butter*	*50 ml*
1	*large onion, diced*	*1*
2	*leeks, chopped (white part only)*	*2*
1	*large potato, peeled and diced*	*1*
1 cup	*fresh mushrooms, sliced*	*250 ml*
1 cup	*carrots, thinly sliced*	*250 ml*
2 cups	*rutabaga, peeled and cubed*	*500 ml*
3 cups	*chicken stock*	*750 ml*
1 tsp	*salt*	*5 ml*
1/4 tsp	*pepper*	*1 ml*
2 1/2 cups	*light cream*	*625 ml*
1/4 cup	*dry white wine*	*50 ml*
2 tbsp	*fresh chives, diced*	*30 ml*

Melt butter in a large heavy pot. Add onion and leeks. Cook until softened. Add potato, mushrooms, carrots and rutabaga. Cook and stir for 3 minutes. Add stock, cover and simmer for 20 to 30 minutes until vegetables are tender. Cool slightly. Purée in blender or food processor until smooth. Return to saucepan and season with salt and pepper. Stir in cream to desired consistency. Add wine. Heat slowly; do not boil. Adjust seasoning. Garnish with chives.
Note: If making ahead or freezing, omit cream, wine and chives; add just before serving.

Lemon Prawn Soup
THAILAND

Serves 8

A pleasant, hot and spicy soup.

7 cups	*chicken broth*	*1.6 l*
2 cups	*straw mushrooms (canned or sliced raw mushrooms)*	*500 ml*
5 tbsp	*Nam Pla fish sauce or anchovy paste*	*75 ml*
10	*lemon leaves, dried*	*10*
5	*6 in/15 cm pieces fresh lemon grass or 2 tbsp/30 ml dried lemon grass*	*5*
2 tbsp	*Nam Prik chili garlic paste or Tabasco sauce to taste*	*30 ml*
2 lbs	*shrimp or prawns, uncooked*	*2 kg*
1	*large tomato, peeled and chopped*	*1*
	coriander - several sprigs	
	hot chili peppers to taste	

Heat chicken stock to boiling. Add mushrooms, Nam Pla, lemon leaves, lemon grass and Nam Prik, and heat through.

Shell and devein shrimp or prawns. Add to stock just before serving. They will turn pink when cooked. Do not overcook, or they will become tough.

Add tomato and put soup in large tureen. Sprinkle coriander on top for garnish.

Note: If using chili peppers, wear rubber gloves while slicing very thinly. Add to soup for last 5 minutes.

Potato and Herb Soup
REPUBLIC OF IRELAND

Serves 6

A hearty cream soup with the delicate flavour of fresh herbs.

3 tbsp	*butter*	*45 ml*
1 cup	*onions, diced*	*250 ml*
1 cup	*green onions, diced*	*250 ml*
3 cups	*potatoes, diced*	*750 ml*
3 cups	*chicken bouillon*	*750 ml*
1	*large sprig fresh parsley*	*1*
1	*sprig fresh rosemary*	*1*
1	*sprig fresh thyme*	*1*
½	*bayleaf*	½
	salt and pepper to taste	
1 cup	*light cream*	*250 ml*
	chopped parsley to garnish	

In a heavy saucepan, heat butter until foaming and toss vegetables until coated. Sprinkle with salt and pepper. Cover and steam gently on a very low heat for 10 to 15 minutes.

Pour in bouillon, add herbs and bring to boil. Cover and simmer gently for approximately 30 minutes or until vegetables are soft. Cool soup slightly. Put through a sieve or blender to purée. Adjust seasonings to taste.

Thin with light cream and return to saucepan and heat through. Garnish with a sprinkling of parsley.

Grandmother's Tomato Soup

QUEBEC

Serves 6

A traditional favourite and so easy to prepare.

3 tbsp	*butter*	*45 ml*
1	*medium onion, finely chopped*	*1*
1	*28 oz can tomatoes, finely chopped*	*875 ml*
½ tsp	*baking soda*	*2 ml*
4 cups	*milk, room temperature*	*1*
1 tsp	*salt*	*5 ml*
1 tsp	*black pepper, freshly ground*	*5 ml*
2 tbsp	*fresh parsley, chopped*	*30 ml*

In a medium saucepan melt butter. Sauté onion until soft and golden. Add tomatoes and simmer for 5 minutes. Add baking soda and stir vigorously to blend. Add milk and salt and pepper to taste. Heat through, but do not boil. Serve immediately with a garnish of fresh parsley.

Wonton Soup

CHINA

Serves 6

Super simple.

	boiling, salted water	
24	*prepared wontons, uncooked (see Fried Wontons for method)*	24
5 cups	*chicken broth*	*1.2 l*
½ tsp	*sesame oil*	*2 ml*
2 tsp	*soy sauce*	*10 ml*
2	*green onions, thinly sliced*	3

Bring salted water to a boil in large saucepan. Add wontons, half at a time and boil about 10 minutes, or until they float, stirring to make sure they do not stick together. Boil 4 minutes more, then drain and rinse under hot water.

Heat chicken broth and season with sesame oil and soy sauce.

Place 4 wontons in each soup bowl and pour broth over. Sprinkle with green onions to serve.

Chirashi Sushi

JAPAN

Serves 6

This cold vegetable-rice salad is terrific - don't be intimidated. It's easy, and can be prepared in advance. Traditionally, in Japan the number nine brings good luck; so try to use nine vegetables.

Rice Mixture:

3 cups	*hot, cooked short grain rice*	*750 ml*
⅓ cup	*white vinegar*	*75 ml*
2 tbsp	*granulated sugar*	*30 ml*
2 tsp	*salt*	*10 ml*

Cool hot rice slightly. Mix vinegar, sugar and salt together until sugar is dissolved. Pour dressing over rice and gently blend. In Japan you would use a fan to finish cooling rice mixture. Set aside.

Vegetable Mixture:

4 oz	*snow peas, slivered*	*125 g*
2	*carrots, peeled and slivered*	*2*
2 in	*piece lotus root, peeled and chopped*	*5 cm*
2 oz	*bamboo shoots*	*50 g*
6	*dried Shiitake mushrooms, reconstituted*	*6*
	additional vegetables, your choice	
15	*small shrimp, cooked*	*15*

Sauce:

½ cup	*dashi or chicken stock*	*125 ml*
½ cup	*soy sauce*	*125 ml*
¼ cup	*sake*	*50 ml*
3 tbsp	*sugar*	*45 ml*

Thoroughly blend sauce ingredients in a saucepan or wok. Cook each vegetable separately in the sauce for approximately 2 minutes, snow peas first, then carrots, lotus root, bamboo shoots, mushrooms, etc. Set aside to cool and toss all vegetables together with shrimp.

To assemble salad, toss rice into vegetable mixture. Make and add the garnish and refrigerate until serving time.

Garnish:

1 tbsp	*sauce from wok*	*15 ml*
2	*eggs*	*2*
2	*green onions, finely chopped*	*2*
2 oz	*red pickled ginger root (Benishoga)*	*50 ml*

Combine sauce from wok and eggs in small bowl. Pour into frying pan and cook as a thin omelet. Slice in strips and set aside. Use to garnish sushi along with onions and pickled gingerroot.

Ota Ika

TONGA

Serves 6

This uncooked appetizer of marinated fish is garnished with chopped tomatoes and shredded cabbage.

1 lb	*halibut, white fish, or shellfish*	*500 g*
2	*juice of 2 lemons*	*2*
½ tsp	*salt*	*2 ml*
1 cup	*coconut cream, fresh or canned*	*250 ml*
⅛ tsp	*chili powder or cayenne pepper*	*pinch*
1	*small onion, finely chopped*	*1*
	chopped tomato and shredded cabbage to garnish	

Cut fish into small cubes. Marinate in lemon juice for 1 hour. Drain.

Mix salt, coconut cream, chili powder or cayenne, and chopped onion. Add to fish.

Arrange attractively on individual plates and garnish with tomato and cabbage.

Fresh Broccoli Salad
NEWFOUNDLAND

Serves 6

Toss this light and crunchy salad with either a creamy or an oil and vinegar style dressing.

4 cups	*broccoli pieces*	*1*
2 slices	*bacon, diced*	*2*
1 cup	*fresh mushrooms, sliced*	*250 ml*

Steam broccoli until tender crisp, about 5 minutes. Run under cold water and drain well.

Chop bacon into tiny pieces and fry until crisp. Drain well on paper towels. Combine broccoli, bacon and mushrooms.

Just before serving, toss with your favourite dressing.

Spinach and Mushroom Salad
ALBERTA

Serves 6

Readily available fresh ingredients make this a year-round salad favourite.

1	*10 oz package fresh spinach, trimmed, washed and dried*	*283 g*
½ cup	*freshly fried bacon, crumbled*	*125 ml*
1 cup	*green onions, sliced*	*250 ml*
2 cups	*fresh mushrooms, sliced*	*500 ml*
¼ cup	*fresh lemon juice*	*50 ml*
½ cup	*olive or canola oil*	*125 ml*
1 tsp	*salt*	*2 ml*
¼ tsp	*black pepper*	*1 ml*
2	*cloves garlic, minced*	2
¼ tsp	*dry mustard*	*1 ml*
¼ tsp	*Tabasco sauce*	*1 ml*
2	*egg yolks, beaten*	2

Place spinach, bacon bits, green onions and mushrooms in a salad bowl. Toss lightly. For dressing, combine remaining eight ingredients in a jar with a tight-fitting lid and shake well.

Just before serving, toss salad with dressing. Store unused dressing in the refrigerator. Allow this dressing to come to room temperature before using.

Herring and Beet Salad

SWEDEN

Serves 8

Serve this do-ahead salad as a starter or as part of a smorgasbord.

Marinade:

1/4 cup	*white vinegar*	*50 ml*
2 tbsp	*water*	*30 ml*
2 tbsp	*sugar*	*30 ml*
1/4 tsp	*white pepper*	*1 ml*

Salad:

2 cups	*cooked beets, cubed*	*500 ml*
1 1/2 cups	*pickled herring, cubed*	*375 ml*
1 1/2 cups	*boiled potatoes, cubed*	*375 ml*
3 tbsp	*dill pickle, chopped*	*45 ml*
2 tbsp	*red onion, chopped*	*30 ml*
	salt and pepper to taste	
2/3 cup	*sour cream or whipped cream*	*175 ml*
	lettuce or spinach leaves	
2	*hard boiled eggs*	2

Combine marinade ingredients in small saucepan. Cook over medium heat, stirring until sugar dissolves. Cool. Pour over beets and refrigerate for 2 hours.

Drain beets; combine with herring, potatoes, pickle, onion, salt and pepper, and enough sour cream or whipped cream to bind. Place lettuce or spinach leaves on individual dishes and mound salad on top.

To garnish: Cut eggs in half lengthwise, crumble yolks on centre of each salad. Cut whites into 6 to 8 strips and arrange attractively around yolks.

Sweet and Sour Salad
PRINCE EDWARD ISLAND

Serves 6

This tangy salad adds a crispy crunch to any meal.

Salad:

1	*romaine lettuce, torn in bite-sized pieces*	*1*
1 cup	*bean sprouts*	*250 ml*
10	*water chestnuts, drained and chopped*	*10*
5	*slices bacon, crisp-cooked and crumbled*	*5*
2	*hard-boiled eggs, finely chopped*	*2*
	salt and pepper to taste	

Dressing:

½ cup	*light vegetable oil*	*125 ml*
¼ cup	*berry sugar*	*50 ml*
3 tbsp	*ketchup*	*45 ml*
2 tbsp	*apple cider vinegar*	*30 ml*
1 tbsp	*onion, minced*	*15 ml*
1 tsp	*Worcestershire sauce*	*5 ml*

Combine dressing ingredients in a jar with a tight-fitting lid and shake well before using. Store in refrigerator if making ahead.

Combine all salad ingredients and season with dash of salt and pepper. Before serving, toss salad with prepared dressing.

Middle Eastern Salad

JORDAN

Serves 6

Fresh herbs and cracked wheat form an interesting make-ahead salad.

1 cup	*bulgur (cracked wheat)*	*250 ml*
2 cups	*cold water*	*500 ml*
3	*medium tomatoes, peeled and chopped*	*3*
1	*cucumber, peeled and chopped*	*1*
1 cup	*fresh parsley, chopped*	*250 ml*
¼ cup	*fresh mint, chopped*	*50 ml*
1 tsp	*fresh oregano, chopped*	*5 ml*
3 tbsp	*green onion, chopped*	*45 ml*
6 tbsp	*olive oil*	*90 ml*
6 tbsp	*fresh lemon juice*	*90 ml*
1 tsp	*salt*	*5 ml*
	black olives and romaine lettuce to garnish	

Soak bulgur in water for 15 minutes. Drain well

Combine with remaining ingredients, except olives and lettuce. Mix, and adjust seasonings to taste. Mound on a serving plate lined with romaine lettuce leaves. Garnish with black olives and serve with pita bread.

Note: Bulgur is available in most bulk and health food stores.

Sour Cream Lettuce Salad

HUNGARY

Serves 6

A zippy salad that teams well with meat or poultry.

1	*head lettuce*	*1*
1 cup	*sour cream or plain yogurt*	*250 ml*
1 tbsp	*apple cider vinegar*	*15 ml*
¼ tsp	*salt*	*1 ml*
⅛ tsp	*pepper*	*pinch*
1	*hard-boiled egg, finely chopped*	*1*

Core lettuce and cut in quarters. Cook in boiling water for 15 minutes, then drain. Rinse with cold water and drain again. Place in a deep-sided, clear serving bowl.

Mix together sour cream, vinegar and spices, adjust seasonings and pour over lettuce. Mix gently.

Top with egg and chill 2 hours before serving.

Fresh Tomato Salad
ONTARIO

Serves 6 to 8

This salad is best prepared a day ahead and stored in the refrigerator.

6	*large tomatoes*	*6*
1	*medium onion, thinly sliced*	*1*
2 tbsp	*fresh parsley, minced*	*30 ml*
1/2 tsp	*basil*	*2 ml*

French Dressing:

1/2 cup	*olive oil*	*125 ml*
1/4 cup	*apple cider vinegar*	*50 ml*
1/2 tsp	*garlic powder*	*2 m*
	salt and pepper to taste	

Place French dressing ingredients into a jar with a tight-fitting lid and shake to mix. Store in refrigerator. Slice tomatoes and arrange decoratively on a platter. Place onion rings at intervals between the tomatoes. Carefully spoon over enough French dressing to coat tomatoes and onions evenly. Sprinkle with basil and parsley. Cover with plastic wrap and store in the refrigerator overnight. Before serving, allow salad to come to room temperature to bring out the flavours.

Marinated Vegetables
BRITISH COLUMBIA

Serves 8

Make an appealing arrangement of marinated fresh seasonal vegetables in a wicker or china basket.

8 cups	*fresh vegetables (carrots, celery, cauliflower, cherry tomatoes, broccoli etc.)*	*2 l*
1 cup	*Italian style salad dressing*	*250 ml*

Chop raw vegetables into bite-size pieces. Toss with salad dressing and refrigerate for at least 4 hours, stirring occasionally.

Drain thoroughly before serving.

Melon Surprise
ICELAND

Serves 8

This rich appetizer is also recommended as a luncheon dish.

2	*melons, cantaloupe or honeydew*	*2*
¼ cup	*mayonnaise*	*50 ml*
1 tbsp	*tomato ketchup*	*15 ml*
½ tsp	*Tabasco sauce*	*2 ml*
2 tbsp	*whipping cream*	*30 ml*
8 oz	*fresh shrimp, cooked*	*250 g*
3 oz	*can mussels*	*85 g*
5 oz	*can lobster meat*	*142 g*
¼ tsp	*salt*	*1 ml*
⅛ tsp	*pepper*	*pinch*
8	*large lettuce leaves*	*8*
8	*sprigs fresh tarragon, or lemon slices*	*8*

Cut melons crosswise into 1 in/2.5 cm thick slices. Remove rind and seeds to form rings. Set aside.

Combine mayonnaise, ketchup, Tabasco and cream. Mix well. Add seafood, and salt and pepper to taste.

Line 8 plates with lettuce leaves, place melon circles on lettuce, fill centre cavity with seafood mixture, and garnish with tarragon or lemon slices.

Serve chilled with melba toast.

Note: For added interest vary the seafood combination.

Lulu Island Cranberry Cooler
BRITISH COLUMBIA

Makes 8 cups/2 L

A refreshing summer drink.

2 cups	*cranberry juice*	*500 ml*
2 cups	*pineapple juice*	*500 ml*
4 cups	*ginger ale*	*1 l*

Combine all ingredients. Pour over a block of ice in a punch bowl and serve immediately.

Fresh cranberry juice:

4 cups	*cranberries*	*1 l*
¼ cup	*water*	*50 ml*
1 cup	*sugar*	*250 ml*

Cook 10 minutes or until soft. Strain and chill.

Main Courses

Barbecued Salmon with Wild Rice Stuffing

BRITISH COLUMBIA

Serves 8

Here is a special marinade for your fresh B.C. salmon. For easy barbecueing encase the fish in chicken wire.

5 lb	*salmon, head and tail removed*	*2.5 kg*

Marinade:

1 cup	*dry white wine*	*250 ml*
½ cup	*fresh lemon juice*	*125 ml*
½ cup	*cooking oil(not olive)*	*125 ml*
2	*cloves garlic, crushed*	*2*
1 tsp	*ground ginger*	*5 ml*
½ tsp	*thyme*	*2 ml*
¼ tsp	*Tabasco sauce*	*1 ml*
1 tsp	*salt*	*5 ml*

Stuffing:

1½ cups	*cooked rice (wild and brown)*	*375 ml*

Garnish:

lemon slices
cherry tomatoes
parsley sprigs

Wash salmon, pat dry. Make diagonal cuts, about ¼ in/6 mm deep, across inside surface of fish.

In saucepan mix marinade ingredients together, heat to boiling, then pour into shallow baking pan and let cool. Lay fish in cooled marinade, refrigerate for 6 hours, turning frequently.

Preheat barbecue. Lightly grease the grill and a piece of chicken wire large enough to encase salmon. Remove fish from marinade. Moisten cooked rice with marinade and stuff fish. Secure with skewers or string. Place fish on wire and fold up to make a basket.

Barbecue 4 in/10 cm from hot coals, 15 minutes per side or until flesh is opaque and flakes readily.

Garnish with lemon slices, cherry tomatoes and parsley.

Nsomba Mangochi
MALAWI

Serves 6

We added mushrooms to this recipe for African lake fish, with delicious results.

1½ lbs	*potatoes or yams*	*750 g*
¼ cup	*milk*	*50 ml*
½ tsp	*salt*	*2 ml*
⅛ tsp	*pepper*	*pinch*
2 tbsp	*butter*	*30 ml*
2 lbs	*chambo, or other white fish*	*1 kg*
1½ cups	*milk*	*375 ml*
½ lb	*mushrooms, sliced*	*250 g*
2 tbsp	*butter*	*30 ml*
1 tbsp	*flour*	*15 ml*
¼ cup	*white wine*	*50 ml*
1	*egg, beaten*	*1*

Cook potatoes and mash with ¼ cup/50 ml milk, seasonings and butter. Set aside and keep warm.

Meanwhile, place fish in saucepan and cover with milk. Simmer gently, without boiling, about 15 to 20 minutes or until tender.

In a small skillet, sauté mushrooms in butter. Add flour and cook, stirring, a further 2 minutes. Gradually add 2 cups/500 ml of liquid in which fish was cooked. Simmer and stir for several more minutes until sauce thickens. Season to taste before adding wine.

Place fish in serving dish, spoon over sauce. Pipe potato around sides of serving dish, brush with beaten egg, and put under broiler to brown lightly.

Fish and Mushroom Roll

U.S.S.R.

Serves 6

This Russian "pirog", served with dill pickles and a salad, makes an excellent luncheon dish.

Filling:

4	*green onions, finely chopped*	*4*
2	*cloves garlic, crushed*	*2*
2 tbsp	*butter*	*30 ml*
1/4 lb	*fresh mushrooms, sliced*	*125 g*
1 tbsp	*fresh dill, chopped*	*15 ml*
1 tbsp	*flour*	*15 ml*
1/2 cup	*fish or chicken stock*	*125 ml*
1/2 tsp	*salt*	*2 ml*
1/4 tsp	*pepper*	*1 ml*
1/8 tsp	*nutmeg*	*pinch*
1 lb	*fresh salmon, haddock or pike, poached and forked into large pieces*	*500 g*
1 1/2 cups	*rice, cooked and cooled*	*375 ml*
3	*hard-boiled eggs, chopped*	*3*
1	*egg yolk, slightly beaten*	*1*

Raised Dough:

1/2 tbsp	*yeast*	*7.5 ml*
2 tbsp	*lukewarm water*	*30 ml*
1/2 cup	*milk, scalded*	*125 ml*
1/4 cup	*butter*	*50 ml*
1/2 tsp	*salt*	*2 ml*
1 tsp	*sugar*	*5 ml*
2 1/2 cups	*flour*	*625 ml*
2	*small eggs, slightly beaten*	*2*

Dissolve yeast in lukewarm water in a large bowl. To scalded milk add butter, salt and sugar; cool to lukewarm before adding to yeast mixture. Stir in ½ cup/125 ml flour, then eggs. Gradually beat in remaining flour, adding enough to make a soft but not sticky dough. Knead 10 minutes or until smooth.

Place dough in a greased bowl. Cover with cloth and let rise in a warm place about 2 hours until double in bulk. The dough is now ready to use.

Filling:

Preheat oven to 375°F/190°C.

Sauté onions and garlic in butter approximately 3 minutes or until tender. Add mushrooms and dill, cook 3 minutes longer.

Stir in flour, stock and seasonings; cook 2 minutes more. Mix in fish and cool.

On a floured pastry cloth, roll out dough into a rectangle 10 x 14 in/25.5 x 36 cm. Place half the rice in middle of dough and spread to within 4 in/10 cm of edge. Spread half the fish mixture on top and cover with chopped egg. Place remaining fish on top of egg, followed by remaining rice. Fold over the long edges of dough and seal both ends by folding and pressing edges together. Place on a greased baking sheet seam side down. Brush surface of dough with egg yolk. Make 5 holes on top to let steam escape.

Bake for 30 to 35 minutes or until golden brown. Cool for 5 minutes before slicing.

Spreewald Style Fish

EAST GERMANY

Serves 4

This fish-vegetable casserole in a yogurt sauce is perfect served with new potatoes which have been rolled in melted butter and fresh dill.

1 lb	*white fish, sole, cod or halibut*	*500 g*
1	*juice from 1 lemon*	*1*
¼ tsp	*salt*	*1 ml*
5	*carrots, sliced*	*5*
1 cup	*celery, sliced*	*250 ml*
2	*small onions, sliced*	*2*
2	*small leeks, thinly sliced*	*2*
2 tbsp	*butter or oil*	*30 ml*
1 cup	*yogurt*	*250 ml*
1 tbsp	*cornstarch*	*15 ml*
½	*large cucumber, sliced*	*½*
1 cup	*fresh parsley, chopped*	*250 ml*

Preheat oven to 350°F/180°C.

Sprinkle fillet with lemon juice and salt; allow fish to marinate for 30 minutes, turning it over once.

Sauté next 4 vegetables in butter or oil for 3 to 5 minutes, stirring frequently. Transfer vegetables to greased baking dish, place fish on top. Mix yogurt and cornstarch and pour over casserole.

Bake, uncovered for 20 minutes. Carefully blend in cucumber and parsley and cook for a further 10 minutes or until fish flakes readily when poked with a fork.

Island Sole

PRINCE EDWARD ISLAND

Serves 6

Crab, shrimp and a subtley flavoured white wine sauce create a special company dish.

½ cup	*flour seasoned with salt and pepper*	*125 ml*
2 lbs	*fresh sole*	*1 kg*
½ cup	*white wine*	*125 ml*
¾ cup	*light cream*	*200 ml*
½ tbsp	*butter*	*7.5 ml*
½ tbsp	*flour*	*7.5 ml*
¼ lb	*fresh crab meat*	*125 g*
¼ lb	*fresh shrimp*	*125 g*
½ cup	*whipping cream, whipped*	*125 ml*
3	*rind of 3 lemons, grated*	*3*

Preheat oven to 450°F/230°C.

Lightly dust sole with seasoned flour and place in shallow greased casserole dish. Pour over wine and light cream. Bake, covered, for 12 minutes or until fish flakes when poked with a fork.

Using a slotted spoon, remove fillets to a platter and keep warm.

Sauce: combine butter and flour in a small saucepan; add liquid from fish and stir over medium heat until smooth. Add crab and shrimp and cook until bubbling. Season with salt and pepper and fold in whipped cream and lemon rind.

Spread sauce over fish and brown under broiler.

Clam Pie

NEW BRUNSWICK

Serves 4 to 6

New Brunswick fishermen bring in a rich harvest of fish and shellfish. A clam catch often finds its way into delectable chowders and casseroles.

	pastry for a 9 in/23 cm double crust pie	
1	*small onion, minced*	*1*
1	*stalk celery, sliced*	*1*
1/4 cup	*butter or margarine*	*50 ml*
1/4 cup	*flour*	*50 ml*
1 cup	*light cream or milk*	*250 ml*
1 cup	*clam liquor (liquid reserved after cooking clams)*	*250 ml*
1/2 tsp	*salt*	*2 ml*
1/8 tsp	*white pepper*	*pinch*
1/8 tsp	*garlic powder (optional)*	*pinch*
3/4 cup	*potatoes, cooked and diced*	*200 ml*
1 1/2 cups	*clams, shelled and cooked or*	*375 ml*
1	*12 oz can clams*	*142 g*
2 tsp	*milk*	*10 ml*

Preheat oven to 450°F/230°C.

Bake bottom pie shell for 5 minutes. Set aside.

Meanwhile, sauté onion and celery in 1 tablespoon/15 ml butter or margarine until soft. Add remaining butter and flour. Cook, stirring, over medium heat for 2 minutes. Gradually add milk and clam liquor and cook gently, stirring constantly, until thickened. Add salt, pepper and garlic powder to taste.

In pie crust lay the potatoes and clams, then cover with sauce. Cover with top crust, trim and seal edges. Cut steam vents in top crust and brush with remaining milk.

Bake in 450°F/230°C oven for 10 minutes. Reduce heat to 350°F/180°C and bake for a further 15 minutes.

Fish Chowder

NOVA SCOTIA

Serves 6

This delicious, easy-to-make soup is hearty, flavourful and colourful.

1 lb	*white fish fillets*	*500 g*
3 tbsp	*butter*	*45 ml*
1	*medium onion, chopped*	*1*
½ cup	*celery, diced*	*125 ml*
2 cups	*potatoes, diced*	*500 ml*
½ cup	*carrots, diced*	*125 ml*
2 cups	*boiling water*	*500 ml*
1 tsp	*pepper*	*pinch*
1	*4 oz can shrimp, drained*	*113 g*
¾ cup	*evaporated milk*	*200 ml*
1 cup	*fresh milk*	*250 ml*
2 tbsp	*fresh parsley, chopped*	*30 ml*

Cut fish into bite-size pieces and set aside. Melt butter in large saucepan, add chopped onion and cook over medium heat until tender but not brown. Add celery, potatoes, carrots, water, salt and pepper. Cover and simmer approximately 15 minutes. Add fish chunks and drained shrimp and cook 15 minutes longer. Add evaporated and fresh milk and heat through but do not boil.

Garnish with fresh, chopped parsley and serve piping hot.

Fish and Tomato Scallop

NEWFOUNDLAND

Serves 6

To a Newfoundlander "fish" means cod, but do not hesitate to substitute your favourite white fish in this versatile recipe.

1 lb	*fresh, uncooked cod, broken in chunks*	*500 g*
1 cup	*breadcrumbs*	*250 ml*
1 cup	*canned tomatoes*	*250 ml*
1	*onion, sliced*	*1*
2 tbsp	*butter*	*30 ml*
½ tsp	*salt*	*2 ml*
¼ tsp	*pepper*	*1 ml*
1	*egg, beaten*	*1*
1 cup	*milk*	*250 ml*

Preheat oven to 350°F/180°C.

Line bottom of 2 qt/2 l casserole with half the breadcrumbs. Add tomatoes, fish and onions. Dot with butter and season. Top with remaining breadcrumbs. Combine beaten egg and milk; pour over fish mixture. Bake, covered for 30 minutes, uncovered for another 30 minutes.

Apricot Chicken

ONTARIO

Serves 6

Use your favourite chicken pieces to make this time-saving and delicious casserole.

3 lb	*frying chicken, cut up*	*1.5 kg*
½ cup	*apricot jam*	*125 ml*
¼ cup	*red French dressing*	*50 ml*
½	*package onion Cup-of-Soup mix*	*15 g*
¼ cup	*water*	*50 ml*

Preheat oven to 350°F/180°C.

Place chicken pieces in a shallow casserole dish. Combine remaining ingredients and pour over chicken. Turn chicken to coat on all sides. Cover casserole and bake for 1½ hours, removing cover for the last 45 minutes.

Yakitori

JAPAN

Serves 6

Use fresh ginger in this chicken-on-skewers dish. It makes all the difference to the flavour.

2 in	*piece fresh ginger, peeled*	*5 cm*
1 lb	*raw, boneless chicken*	*500 g*
3	*leeks, or your choice of vegetable*	*3*
½ cup	*sake*	*125 ml*
½ cup	*soy sauce*	*125 ml*
1 tbsp	*sugar*	*15 ml*
1	*clove garlic, crushed*	*1*
	vegetable oil	

Finely grate or chop ginger. Cut chicken into bite-sized pieces. Cut white part of leeks into ½ in/2 cm pieces. Mix sake, soy sauce, sugar, garlic and ginger, and pour over chicken. Marinate for 15 minutes.

Alternate 3 pieces of chicken with 2 pieces of leek on oiled skewers. Brush with marinade and broil five minutes. Rebaste with marinade, turn them over, and broil approximately 5 minutes longer, or until done.

Chicken Paprika

HUNGARY

Serves 6

Traditionally, dumplings are served with this famed Hungarian dish.

3 lbs	*chicken pieces*	*1.5 kg*
2 tbsp	*butter*	*30 ml*
2	*onions, sliced*	*2*
1 cup	*water*	*250 ml*
2 tsp	*paprika*	*10 ml*
1 tsp	*salt*	*5 ml*
¼ tsp	*pepper*	*1 ml*
2 tbsp	*flour*	*30 ml*
1	*green pepper, sliced*	*1*
2	*medium tomatoes, quartered*	*2*
½ cup	*sour cream*	*125 ml*

Wash chicken pieces and pat dry with paper towel. Melt butter in large skillet. Cook chicken over medium heat about 10 minutes until browned on all sides. Remove chicken from pan and set aside. Retain fat in frying pan.

Brown onion in remaining fat until tender and golden. Remove onion, set aside. Turn skillet off.

Drain off excess fat. In jar with tightly fitting lid combine water, paprika, salt, pepper and flour. Shake well before pouring into skillet. Reheat, stirring to blend. Add chicken pieces, then onion and just bring to the boil. Reduce heat, cover and simmer for 30 minutes.

Add green pepper and tomatoes. Continue to cook about 20 minutes, or until chicken is tender.

Remove chicken and vegetables, arrange on warm serving platter. Turn heat to very low and add sour cream to gravy in skillet. Stir to blend and heat through without boiling. Pour gravy over chicken or serve separately.

Ginger Braised Chicken

CHINA

Serves 6

With just plain rice this chicken-vegetable dish is a meal in itself.

3 oz	*dried Chinese black mushrooms*	*93 g*
3 lb	*chicken*	*1.5 kg*
1 tbsp	*cornstarch*	*15 ml*
½ cup	*peanut oil*	*125 ml*
3	*stalks celery, cut diagonally*	*3*
	in 1 in/2.5 cm strips	*3*
1	*green pepper, cut in strips*	*1*
2	*medium carrots, cut in coins*	*2*
½ cup	*light soy sauce*	*125 ml*
¼ cup	*rice wine*	*50 ml*
2 tbsp	*sugar*	*30 ml*
2 in	*piece ginger root, peeled and slivered*	*5 cm*
2	*green onions, finely chopped*	*2*

Soak mushrooms in hot water for 30 minutes. Drain, squeezing out excess moisture.

Steam or boil chicken until tender. Cool, and cut into serving size pieces.

Heat peanut oil in wok or pan. Coat chicken pieces lightly with cornstarch and fry a few minutes until golden. Set chicken aside and add celery, green pepper and carrots. Stir fry about 2 minutes until lightly cooked. Drain off oil. Return chicken to pan and add remaining ingredients, including mushrooms. Cover and steam gently 5 to 10 minutes. With a slotted spoon, place chicken and vegetables on serving dish leaving sauce in wok. Thicken sauce with 1 tsp cornstarch and simmer a further 5 minutes. Pour sauce over chicken.

Flemish Waterzooi

BELGIUM

Serves 6

This hearty chicken-vegetable soup is one of the few regional dishes to be found on menus in the most exalted restaurants in Belgium. Here is our variation.

¾ lb	*leeks*	*375 g*
¾ lb	*celery*	*375 g*
½ lb	*mushrooms*	*250 g*
8 cups	*water*	*2 l*
½ lb	*veal stewmeat, diced*	*250 g*
¼ cup	*butter*	*50 ml*
2 lbs	*chicken pieces*	*1 kg*
1 tsp	*salt*	*5 ml*
¼ tsp	*pepper*	*1 ml*
4	*egg yolks*	*4*
¾ cup	*heavy cream*	*200 ml*
½ cup	*fresh parsley, chopped*	*125 ml*
1	*lemon, sliced*	*1*

Cut vegetables into bite-size pieces and set aside. Reserve green part of leeks and celery leaves for the broth.

Combine water, veal and vegetable greens in a large saucepan. Bring to boil and simmer for 30 minutes.

Meanwhile, put butter in a large pan, add chicken pieces, leeks, celery, mushrooms, salt and pepper. Sauté, uncovered, for about 15 minutes, stirring frequently to prevent burning.

Strain veal broth and add to chicken and vegetables. Cover and cook about 45 minutes or until chicken is tender.

Remove and set aside vegetable pieces and chicken. Debone chicken. Whirl broth in a blender, if necessary.

In bottom of a large casserole or saucepan, mix egg yolks and cream using a wire whisk. Add broth, chicken meat, vegetables and chopped parsley. Return to heat and warm through; do not boil. Adjust seasonings. Serve hot in large bowls along with country-style bread. Garnish with a slice of fresh lemon.

Paella
SPAIN

Serves 8 to 10

This meal-in-a-dish is great for large parties, especially when served with garlic bread and salad. It can easily be doubled.

3 tbsp	*olive oil*	*45 ml*
1½ lbs	*chicken pieces*	*750 g*
1	*medium onion, chopped*	*1*
2	*cloves garlic, crushed*	*2*
½ lb	*tomatoes, chopped*	*250 g*
3 cups	*water or chicken broth*	*750 ml*
1 tsp	*salt*	*5 ml*
¼ tsp	*pepper*	*1 ml*
1½ cups	*uncooked rice*	*375 ml*
⅛ tsp	*saffron or turmeric*	*pinch*
½ lb	*lobster meat*	*250 g*
1 lb	*shrimp or prawns*	*500 g*
1	*10 oz package frozen peas*	*284 g*
2 oz	*pimentos*	*50 ml*
8	*cooked mussels or clams in shells*	*8*

Heat oil in Dutch oven and fry chicken until brown on all sides. Remove chicken; fry chopped onion, garlic and tomato pieces. Return chicken to pan, add water or broth and season with salt and pepper. Simmer gently for 15 minutes.

Add rice and saffron, blended with a little broth and cook for a further 10 minutes.

Stir in lobster, shrimp and peas, and cook for 10 more minutes or until all liquid is absorbed and meat is cooked and tender. Adjust seasonings.

Serve garnished with pimentos and mussels or clams in shells.

This dish can also be cooked in the oven. Allow at least 1 hour at 350°F/180°C.

Note: To prepare ahead for freezer storage, do not add pimentos and shellfish until reheating.

Thai Chicken Curry

THAILAND

Serves 8

Homemade curry paste makes this chicken special.

4	*boneless chicken breasts, in bite-size pieces*	4

Curry paste:

5 tbsp	*Nam Prik chili garlic paste or 1 tsp/5 ml dried red chilies*	*75 ml*
4 tbsp	*crushed garlic*	*60 ml*
4 tbsp	*Chinese parsley, chopped*	*60 ml*
4 tbsp	*dried, shredded lemon grass*	*60 ml*
8	*slices dried Kar, or ginger root*	*8*
6 tbsp	*onion, chopped*	*90 ml*
1 tsp	*salt*	*5 ml*
1 tsp	*rind of Makrut, chopped or grated lime peel*	*5 ml*

Chicken Sauce:

6 cups	*coconut milk, fresh or canned*	*1.5 L*
4	*dried lemon leaves*	*4*
2 tbsp	*sugar*	*30 ml*
2 tbsp	*Nam Pla fish sauce or anchovy paste*	*30 ml*
½ tsp	*salt*	*2 ml*
1	*8 oz can bamboo shoots, drained and sliced*	*227 ml*
½ cup	*basil, chopped*	*125 ml*
1 lb	*frozen peas*	*500 g*

Optional:

½ cup	*red and green chilies, cut very thinly, or 2 tbsp/30 ml paprika*	*125 ml*

In a blender, combine all curry paste ingredients and mix thoroughly. This can be made a few days ahead and stored in refrigerator, to develop a more subtle flavour. Unused paste can be frozen.

In a bowl mix curry paste and chicken pieces. Marinate for at least 30 minutes.

Heat 4 cups coconut milk to boiling, add marinated chicken pieces and stir, bringing back to boil. Reduce heat and cook about 15 minutes, or until chicken is tender. Do not overcook. At this stage curried chicken may be frozen or refrigerated for a few days to mellow.

Reheat, adding lemon leaves, sugar, Nam Pla, salt, remaining coconut milk, bamboo shoots and basil leaves. Cook 10 minutes, add peas and chilies and cook another 5 minutes.

Transfer curried chicken to heated serving bowl, and if desired garnish with Chinese parsley. Serve with rice.

Roast Turkey and Gravy

UNITED STATES OF AMERICA

Serves 8

Simple roast turkey with cornbread stuffing is a Thanksgiving classic.

1	*12 lb turkey*	*6 kg*
	cornbread stuffing	
3 tbsp	*butter, melted*	*45 ml*
3 tbsp	*flour*	*45 ml*
1 cup	*water*	*250 ml*
	salt & pepper to taste	

Preheat oven to 325°F/165°C.

Stuff turkey, and place breast side up in shallow roasting pan. Brush with melted butter, wrap in foil and roast, basting occasionally for 5 to 6 hours or until meat thermometer registers 185°F/85°C. Foil may be removed for last hour of roasting to brown the bird. Let stand 15 minutes before carving.

Gravy: Remove fat from roasting pan, leaving drippings. Stir in flour and gradually add water. On stove top, bring to a boil, stirring constantly, and cook until gravy thickens. Add salt and pepper to taste.

Roast Duck
SASKATCHEWAN

Serves 6

A successfully cooked duck features moist meat and crisp skin.

2	*5 lb ducks*	*5 kg*
1 tsp	*salt*	*5 ml*
½ tsp	*pepper*	*2 ml*
1	*large apple, quartered*	*1*
1	*large onion, quartered*	*1*
2	*celery sticks, sliced*	*2*
2	*carrots, sliced in coins*	*2*
1 cup	*apple juice or cider*	*250 ml*

Preheat oven to 325°F/165°C.

Wash ducks thoroughly, pat dry to ensure crisp skin, and sprinkle insides with salt and pepper. Place apple, onion, celery and carrot segments inside each cavity. Place ducks on rack in a large roasting pan. Prick skin with a fork - do not puncture meat. Pour apple juice or cider over ducks. Roast, uncovered, for approximately 2 hours. After first 20 minutes of cooking prick skin again. Baste occasionally with apple and pan juices, pouring off excess fat as it accumulates.

When roasting is complete, remove birds from the oven and let sit for 10 minutes before carving.

Glazed Cornish Game Hens

REPUBLIC OF IRELAND

Serves 8

A recipe that makes a delightful company dish.

½ cup	*orange juice*	*125 ml*
1 tbsp	*lemon juice*	*15 ml*
¼ cup	*apricot jam*	*50 ml*
⅓ cup	*raisins*	*75 ml*
⅓ cup	*orange juice*	*75 ml*
1½ tsp	*butter*	*7 ml*
¾ cup	*fresh mushrooms, sliced*	*200 ml*
⅓ cup	*celery, chopped*	*75 ml*
½	*apple, unpeeled and diced*	*½*
2 cups	*rice, cooked*	*500 ml*
½ tsp	*cinnamon*	*2 ml*
¼ tsp	*nutmeg*	*1 ml*
¼ tsp	*ginger*	*1 ml*
¼ tsp	*salt*	*1 ml*
4	*Cornish game hens*	*4*

To make glaze: combine first three ingredients, stir well and set aside.

To prepare stuffing: soak raisins in ⅓ cup/75 ml orange juice. Set aside. Melt butter in small pan, add mushrooms, celery and apple. Sauté lightly. In a medium bowl combine rice with next four spices. Blend in sautéed fruit and vegetables plus raisin mixture. Stir well. Divide stuffing between four hens.

Preheat oven to 350°F/180°C.

Arrange stuffed hens in a roasting pan, drizzle with glaze and cover with foil. Bake for 60 minutes, basting frequently. Remove foil and bake a further 30 minutes, basting occasionally.

Allow hens to sit for 5 minutes at room temperature. Cut each hen in half to serve.

Partridge with Cabbage
QUEBEC

Serves 6 to 8

Partridge, Cornish game hens, or pheasant can be used to make this simple casserole.

½ lb	*salt pork, diced*	*250 g*
4	*partridges, cut in half*	*4*
1	*large onion, chopped*	*1*
1	*large cabbage, coarsely sliced*	*1*
½ cup	*red wine*	*125 ml*
	salt and pepper to taste	

Preheat oven to 325°F/165°C.

Sauté diced salt pork in a heavy pan until crisp. Remove pork and set aside. Sauté birds in the fat until golden. Remove birds and pat with paper towel to remove excess fat. Add onions to pan and cook until transparent.

Boil cabbage for 10 minutes. Drain.

Cover bottom of a large casserole with 1 cup/250 ml cooked cabbage. Arrange birds, onions and half the amount of salt pork pieces, on the bed of cabbage. Cover with remaining cabbage. Pour wine evenly over casserole and sprinkle with salt and pepper to taste. Cook in oven for 2 hours; covered the first hour, uncovered the second hour.

Barbecued Pork

CHINA

Serves 6

A rich, dark, sweet and sour sauce makes this pork so tasty!

2 lbs	*boneless pork (butt or tenderloin)*	*1 kg*
2	*cloves garlic, crushed*	*2*
1 in	*piece ginger root, peeled & grated*	*2.5 cm*
1	*green onion, thinly sliced*	*1*
2 tbsp	*sherry*	*30 ml*
2 tbsp	*hoi sin sauce*	*30 ml*
½ cup	*soy sauce*	*125 ml*
¼ cup	*brown sugar*	*50 ml*
½ tsp	*five-spice*	*2 ml*
2 tbsp	*honey*	*30 ml*
2 tbsp	*water*	*30 ml*

Cut pork into even strips, about 2 in/5 cm by ¾ in/1.8 cm.

Mix remaining ingredients and marinate pork at least 1 hour. Place pork and marinade in baking pan, and roast for 1½ hours at 325°F/165°C, basting frequently. Sauce will be dark and syrupy. Add water if it becomes too dry.

Serve warm or cold, with main meal or as an appetizer with a soy sauce dip.

Note: Five-spice is a mixture of fennel or anise, ginger, licorice root, cinnamon and cloves; it is available in specialty stores.

Loma de Puerco

PANAMA

Serves 6

The combination of lemon, garlic, onion and pimento gives this pork dish a truly distinctive flavour.

2½ lb	*pork loin*	*1.25 kg*
1 cup	*water*	*250 ml*
1 tsp	*salt*	*5 ml*
1	*juice of 1 large lemon*	*1*
4	*cloves garlic, slivered*	*4*
1	*medium onion, sliced*	*1*
1	*2 oz jar pimento, undrained*	*57 ml*
1 tsp	*garlic powder*	*5 ml*
3 tbsp	*dark rum*	*45 ml*

Marinate pork in water, salt and lemon juice for 3 hours or overnight. Remove pork from marinade and stud with garlic slivers. Cover pork with onion slices and pimento and sprinkle with garlic powder. Add rum to marinade, pour over pork and allow to stand for another 30 minutes.

Preheat oven to 375°F/190°C.

Place pork and marinade in a covered roasting pan and bake for 3 hours, basting frequently.

West German Pork

WEST GERMANY

Serves 6 to 8

This dinner party dish is good with red cabbage and new potatoes.

2 lb	*loin or boneless leg of pork*	*1 kg*
1 cup	*water*	*250 ml*
1 cup	*white wine*	*250 ml*
1 tbsp	*apple cider vinegar*	*15 ml*
4	*bay leaves*	*4*
½ tsp	*salt*	*2 ml*
¼ tsp	*pepper*	*1 ml*
1 tbsp	*flour*	*15 ml*
1 cup	*madeira wine*	*250 ml*
3	*medium apples, peeled and sliced*	*3*

Preheat oven to 350°F/180°C.

Place pork in roasting pan along with water, white wine, vinegar, bay leaves, salt and pepper. Cook for approximately 1½ hours or until pork is tender and thoroughly cooked. Remove and slice the meat, arranging it attractively on a platter. Keep warm.

Mix flour with 2 tbsp/10 ml madeira wine. Add, with remaining madeira, to juices in pan. Adjust seasoning and stir sauce over medium heat until slightly thickened. Spoon sauce over meat slices.

Garnish: Cook apples in separate pan in the oven for about 10 minutes. Arrange around meat.

Pork Stuffed Cabbage
ONTARIO

Serves 6

Our testers agreed that this tasty dish was suitable for both family and company dining.

1 lb	*ground pork*	*500 g*
1	*medium cabbage*	*1*
1½ cups	*fresh breadcrumbs*	*375 ml*
2 tbsp	*butter, melted*	*30 ml*
¼ cup	*onion, chopped*	*50 ml*
¼ cup	*celery, chopped*	*50 ml*
1 tsp	*salt*	*5 ml*
1 tsp	*savory*	*5 ml*
1 tsp	*thyme*	*5 ml*
½ tsp	*pepper*	*2 ml*
1	*egg, beaten*	*1*
4	*slices bacon*	*4*
1	*14 oz can tomato sauce*	*398 ml*

In a small frying pan partially cook ground pork for 2 to 3 minutes. Set aside.

Remove centre of cabbage (save for coleslaw), leaving a wall of approximately 1 in/2.5 cm all around. Remove a slice from the bottom so cabbage will sit flat. Blanch cabbage in boiling water for 3 to 5 minutes. Drain thoroughly. Set aside.

Preheat oven to 350°F/180°C.

To prepare breadcrumb mixture, melt butter in a saucepan; add onions and celery. Sauté vegetables for 2 minutes before adding breadcrumbs, seasonings and beaten egg. Stir in partially cooked pork. Pack stuffing mixture tightly into centre of the cabbage.

Lay 2 slices of bacon in bottom of Dutch oven and place cabbage on top. Cover with 2 slices of bacon. Pour tomato sauce over cabbage and bacon. Cover and bake for 2 to 2½ hours.

Tortang Baysanan
PHILLIPINES

Serves 4 to 6

For a luncheon or light supper, serve this flavourful omelet with toast and a tossed salad.

2	*cloves garlic, crushed*	*2*
1	*medium onion, chopped*	*1*
2	*medium potatoes, peeled and finely chopped*	*2*
2	*medium tomatoes, chopped*	*2*
2 tbsp	*vegetable oil*	*30 ml*
1 tsp	*salt*	*5 ml*
¼ tsp	*pepper*	*1 ml*
1 lb	*ground pork*	*500 g*
6	*large eggs*	*6*
2	*medium red peppers, chopped*	*2*
1 tbsp	*vegetable oil*	*15 ml*

In a skillet, sauté garlic, onion, and potatoes in oil. Add tomatoes, season with salt and pepper. Add ground pork, mix thoroughly, cover, and cook about 8 minutes until pork is well done. Set aside to cool slightly and pour off excess fat.

Beat eggs thoroughly. Fold in pork mixture and red pepper. Heat remaining oil in skillet, tipping to grease sides and bottom evenly. Turn heat to low and add pork-egg mixture. Cook over low heat until well set and firm on sides. Loosen sides of omelet with spatula and slide onto ovenproof plate. If top of omelet is too moist, place under broiler until set.

Nasi-Goreng, Shellane Style
INDONESIA

Serves 4

An attractive meal in a dish.

¼ cup	*vegetable oil*	*50 ml*
4	*cloves garlic, crushed*	*4*
2	*eggs, beaten*	*2*
1 cup	*ham, chopped*	*250 ml*
1 cup	*prawns or shrimp*	*250 ml*
¼ tsp	*salt*	*1 ml*
3 cups	*rice, cooked and chilled*	*750 ml*
1 cup	*frozen peas, thawed*	*250 ml*
1	*green onion, finely chopped*	*1*
2 tbsp	*light soya sauce*	*30 ml*
1	*medium onion, sliced and fried till brown and crispy*	*1*
3	*fresh red chilies, seeds removed and cut into small pieces*	*3*
	a few slices of cucumber or lettuce	

Heat cooking oil in frying pan. Fry garlic, beaten eggs, ham and prawns for a few minutes until egg is set, stirring constantly. Add salt, rice, peas, green onion, and soya sauce. Fry for about 5 more minutes, stirring constantly.

Serve with browned onion and red chilies sprinkled on top. Add cucumber or lettuce if desired.

Swedish Glazed Ham

SWEDEN

Serves 12

A tasty mustard glaze makes this ham a little different.

12 lb	*ham*	*6 kg*

Cook ham according to personal preference. For the last 40 minutes apply glaze and cook in 350°F/180°C oven until nicely browned.

Glaze:

1	*egg white, beaten*	*1*
1 tbsp	*dry mustard*	*15 ml*
1 tbsp	*sugar*	*15 ml*
	fine breadcrumbs	

Mix beaten egg white, mustard and sugar and brush on partially cooked ham. Press on a generous sprinkling of fine breadcrumbs.

Garnish:

parsley sprigs
cooked, pitted prunes
cooked apple sections

Garnish platter with parsley, prunes and apple sections, and cover ham knuckle with paper frill. Serve warm or cold.

English Pot Roast

GREAT BRITAIN

Serves 6

This flavourful meat dish is both nutritious and economical - great with baked potatoes.

3 tbsp	*beef dripping*	*45 ml*
2½ lb	*rolled beef brisket*	*1.25 kg*
4	*onions, peeled and chopped*	*4*
4	*carrots, peeled and sliced*	*4*
1	*small rutabaga, peeled and cubed*	*1*
½ lb	*small fresh mushrooms*	*250 g*
1	*10 oz can beef broth or consommé*	284 ml
⅛ tsp	*thyme*	*pinch*
1 tbsp	*fresh parsley, chopped*	*15 ml*
1	*small bay leaf*	*1*
1 tsp	*salt*	*5 ml*
⅛ tsp	*pepper*	*pinch*

Preheat oven to 300°F/150°C.

Melt dripping in large, thick pot. Add meat and brown on all sides. Remove meat and set aside. Lightly sauté vegetables. Remove, using a slotted spoon and set aside. Remove fat from pot. Return meat and vegetables, add broth, herbs, salt and pepper. Cover and cook in oven approximately 3 hours (alternatively, simmer on stove top).

Remove meat and vegetables and arrange attractively on platter. Reduce cooking liquid slightly and adjust seasonings. Thicken gravy with cornstarch if desired, and serve with the meat and vegetables.

Roast Caribou
NORTHWEST TERRITORIES

Serves 6 to 8

Beef can be substituted for caribou when preparing this tasty dish.

4 - 5 lb	*caribou roast*	*2 - 2.5 kg*
1	*10 oz can mushroom soup*	*284 ml*
1	*package dry onion soup mix*	*66 g*
¾ cup	*water*	*200 ml*

Allow meat to come to room temperature.

Preheat oven to 350°F/180°C.

To make gravy, combine next 3 ingredients thoroughly. Tear off piece of aluminum foil large enough to wrap meat loosely with shiny side towards meat. Lay foil in roasting pan, place meat on top, and pour gravy over meat. Fold foil around meat, being careful to seal the package completely. Foil should loosely surround meat to allow juices to form a gravy. Cook in oven for 30 minutes per lb/500 g. Slice meat thinly and serve gravy in a separate bowl.

Tangy Alberta Shortribs
ALBERTA

Serves 6

Shortribs, or spareribs can be used in this versatile recipe.

4 lbs	*shortribs*	*2 kg*
½ cup	*oil*	*125 ml*
½ cup	*vinegar*	*125 ml*
¼ lb	*onions, chopped*	*125 g*
1	*14 oz bottle tomato ketchup*	*375 ml*
1 tbsp	*rum*	*15 ml*
1 tbsp	*sugar*	*15 ml*
1½ tbsp	*Worcestershire sauce*	*22 ml*
⅛ tsp	*pepper*	*pinch*
⅛ tsp	*thyme*	*pinch*

To make sauce, mix oil, vinegar and chopped onions in a blender. Add remaining ingredients and blend thoroughly. Store in refrigerator if not using immediately.

Trim fat from shortribs and place in large saucepan. Cover with water and simmer gently for 1½ hours. Drain. Remove excess fat. Preheat oven to 350°F/180°C.

Place ribs in a large casserole dish, cover with sauce and bake, covered, for approximately one hour.

Karelian Stew

FINLAND

Serves 6

A variety of meats make this a nourishing casserole for cold, crisp days.

1 lb	*stewing beef*	*500 g*
½ lb	*lamb stew piece*	*250 g*
1	*small calf kidney*	*1*
¼ lb	*calf liver*	*125 g*
½ lb	*pork pieces*	*250 g*
6	*whole allspice*	*6*
1 tbsp	*salt*	*15 ml*
	water	
2	*onions, quartered*	*2*
8	*carrots, sliced*	*8*
3 tbsp	*cornstarch*	*45*

Preheat oven to 375°F/190°C.

Rinse meat in cold water and cut into bite-size pieces. Arrange meat and seasonings in layers, pork on top, in an oven-proof casserole dish. Add water to barely cover meat. Bake, uncovered, for 30 minutes. Reduce heat to 325°F/165°C. Add onions and carrots, cover, and simmer for 3 hours.

Thicken gravy with cornstarch before serving with mashed potatoes and vegetables.

Lu Pulu

TONGA

Serves 6

This beef-vegetable roll was rated excellent by our testers.

10	*young taro plant leaves or cabbage leaves*	*10*
2 lbs	*sirloin, cut into $\frac{1}{2}$ in/1.3 cm cubes*	*1 kg*
2	*medium onions, thinly sliced*	*2*
2	*medium tomatoes, chopped in small pieces*	*2*
$1\frac{1}{2}$ cups	*coconut cream, fresh or canned*	*375 ml*
$\frac{1}{2}$ tsp	*salt*	*2 ml*

Preheat oven to 350°F/180°C.

Clean leaves and arrange them on sheet of foil, overlapping so that they will hold all the other ingredients.

Place onions, tomatoes and beef on leaves. Pour coconut cream over all and sprinkle with salt. Bring leaves together, wrapping ingredients so liquid will not spill out. Wrap in the foil.

Bake in preheated oven about 2 hours or until meat is tender.

Bul-Ko-Kee

SOUTH KOREA

Serves 8

This beef recipe is so popular in Korea that it is widely considered to be the national meat dish.

2 lbs	*sirloin, rib or flank steak*	*1 kg*
6 tbsp	*brown sugar, loosely packed*	*90 ml*
1 cup	*soy sauce*	*250 ml*
$\frac{1}{8}$ tsp	*salt*	*pinch*
$\frac{1}{8}$ tsp	*pepper*	*pinch*
$\frac{1}{2}$ cup	*roasted sesame seeds, ground*	*125 ml*
$\frac{1}{2}$ cup	*sesame oil*	*125 ml*
3	*cloves garlic, crushed*	*3*
4	*green onions, finely chopped*	*4*

Cut the steak on the bias into wafer thin strips. Score each piece with an X.

Combine sugar, soy sauce, salt, pepper, half the sesame seeds, oil, garlic and onions. Add beef strips and mix well. Set meat mixture aside at room temperature for 2 hours, basting and turning the meat frequently.

Broil beef strips for 5 to 8 minutes or until meat is cooked through and evenly browned. Beef may also be sautéed in a little sesame oil until browned.

Remove from heat, sprinkle with remaining sesame seeds and serve at once.

Sukiyaki

JAPAN

Serves 6

Sukiyaki is always prepared at the table in front of the guests and is served with rice.

2 lbs	*lean beef, very thinly sliced*	*1 kg*
½ lb	*spinach, cleaned and trimmed*	*250 g*
1	*large onion, thinly sliced*	*1*
1	*7 oz container fresh Shirataki noodles*	*200 g*
1 or 2	*tofu cakes*	*1 or 2*
12	*large, fresh mushrooms, stems removed*	*12*

Attractively arrange the above ingredients on a large platter.

1 tbsp	*vegetable oil*	*15 ml*
6	*raw eggs, optional*	*6*
6 cups	*hot, cooked rice*	*1.5 l*

Sauce:

1 cup	*water*	*250 ml*
½ cup	*soy sauce*	*125 ml*
½ cup	*sake*	*125 ml*
2 tbsp	*sugar*	*30 ml*

Combine sauce ingredients in a small pitcher.

Assemble all ingredients at the table, and heat oil in an electric skillet or chafing dish. Brown half the meat. Add half the vegetables, noodles and tofu, plus ¼ cup/50 ml sauce. Cook approximately 2 minutes. Add a little more sauce, mix, and offer guests to help themselves with chopsticks. Repeat process.

Traditionally, each guest has a slightly beaten egg in a small bowl. The cooked meat and vegetables are dipped into the egg before eating.

Carpet Bag Steak
AUSTRALIA

Serves 8

This oyster-stuffed steak is something a bit different.

4 lb	*piece fillet steak*	*2 kg*
¼ cup	*butter*	*50 ml*
16	*oysters*	*16*
¼ lb	*mushrooms, sliced*	*125 g*
1 cup	*breadcrumbs*	*250 ml*
1 tbsp	*fresh parsley, chopped*	*15 ml*
	grated rind of ½ lemon	
¼ tsp	*salt*	*1 ml*
⅛ tsp	*pepper*	*pinch*
⅛ tsp	*paprika or garlic powder*	*pinch*
1	*small egg*	*1*

Preheat oven to 350°F/180°C.

Trim steak and cut small pockets in it, one for each person.

Heat butter in saucepan and gently fry oysters and mushrooms for 5 minutes. Transfer to a mixing bowl and combine with breadcrumbs, parsley, lemon rind and seasonings. Beat egg, then stir into stuffing mixture.

Place stuffing into the pockets in the meat and tie or skewer edges together. Roast in oven for 40 to 60 minutes, depending on desired doneness.

Variation: For barbecueing or broiling, use individual steaks.

Tamale Pie

MEXICO

Serves 6

Adjust the amount of chili powder to suit your taste when preparing this family-style casserole.

1 lb	*ground beef*	*500 g*
2	*medium onions, chopped*	*2*
1	*large green pepper, chopped*	*1*
2	*8 oz cans tomato sauce*	*500 ml*
1	*12 oz can whole kernel corn, drained*	*375 ml*
¼ cup	*pitted ripe olives, chopped*	*50 ml*
1	*clove garlic, crushed*	*1*
1 tbsp	*sugar*	*15 ml*
1 tsp	*salt*	*5 ml*
2 tsp	*chili powder*	*10 ml*
2 cups	*Monterey Jack cheese, grated*	*500 ml*

Cornmeal topping:

¾ cup	*yellow cornmeal*	*200 ml*
½ tsp	*salt*	*2 ml*
2 cups	*water*	*500 ml*
1 tbsp	*butter*	*15 ml*

Sauté meat, onion and green pepper until vegetables are tender and meat is no longer pink. Add next 8 ingredients, stir to blend, and simmer 20 minutes.

Add cheese and stir until melted. Pour into a 9 in/23 cm square baking pan.

Preheat oven to 375°F/190°C.

Topping: In a saucepan, stir cornmeal and salt into cold water. Cook over medium heat, stirring, for approximately 3 minutes until thick. Add butter. Mix well before spooning over meat mixture, making narrow strips with dough. Bake for 40 minutes until top is browned.

So'o-Iosopy
PARAGUAY

Serves 6

An unusual thick meat soup, frequently served as a main dish.

1 lb	*finely ground meat*	*500 g*
2 tbsp	*uncooked rice*	*30 ml*
3 tbsp	*vegetable oil*	*45 ml*
1	*medium onion, sliced*	*1*
1	*sweet red pepper, sliced*	*1*
1	*large tomato, finely chopped*	*1*
3	*green onions, sliced*	*3*
1 tbsp	*flour*	*15 ml*
8 cups	*water*	*2 l*
1 tsp	*salt*	*5 ml*
½ tsp	*oregano*	*2 ml*
¼ cup	*fresh parsley, finely chopped*	*50 ml*

Combine meat and rice. Run through food processor, or pound until a paste-like consistency is achieved.

Heat oil in skillet, add sliced onion and red pepper and sauté until tender but not brown. Add tomato and green onions and cook 5 minutes longer. Remove from heat and allow to cool slightly.

In a large saucepan combine meat paste and tomato-onion mixture. Dissolve flour in 8 cups/2 l water and add to mixture. Stir thoroughly. Cook over medium heat, stirring constantly, for 15 to 20 minutes.

Season to taste with salt and oregano, and serve garnished with parsley.

Roast Stuffed Leg of Lamb

NEW ZEALAND

Serves 6

Famous New Zealand lamb, a hint of pineapple and succulent roast potatoes.

4-5 lb	*leg of lamb, slit for stuffing*	*2.5 kg*
½ tsp	*salt*	*2 ml*
⅛ tsp	*pepper*	*pinch*
2 tbsp	*butter*	*30 ml*
1 cup	*fine, soft breadcrumbs*	*250 ml*
½ cup	*celery, chopped*	*125 ml*
½ tsp	*salt*	*2 ml*
½ cup	*crushed pineapple, drained thoroughly*	*125 ml*
1	*large clove garlic, quartered*	*1*
1 tbsp	*butter*	*15 ml*
1 tbsp	*fresh lemon juice*	*15 ml*
¼ tsp	*ground ginger*	*1 ml*
6	*potatoes, halved*	*6*
½ cup	*red or blackcurrant jelly*	*125 ml*

Preheat oven to 325°F/165°C.

Have your butcher slit a pocket in the leg of lamb. Rub outside of lamb with salt and pepper. Melt butter and combine breadcrumbs, celery, salt and crushed pineapple. Stuff pocket of lamb with mixture and fasten with skewers. Make 4 small slits in lamb and insert garlic quarters. Rub lamb with butter; sprinkle with lemon juice and ginger. Place in greased roasting pan and surround with halved potatoes coated with oil or butter. Roast for 2 hours, or until lamb and potatoes are cooked to desired "doneness". Baste potatoes occasionally, adding extra butter if necessary. During last 15 minutes, glaze roast with ½ cup/125 ml currant jelly which has been heated slightly.

Remove garlic cloves before carving.

Roast Lamb with Potatoes
GREECE

Serves 6

Lemon-basil flavoured potatoes are delicious with a simple lamb roast.

4 lb	*leg or shoulder of lamb*	*2 kg*
2	*cloves garlic, slivered*	*2*
1	*onion, sliced in rings*	*1*
2 tbsp	*fresh lemon juice*	*30 ml*
8	*medium potatoes, peeled and halved*	*8*
2 tsp	*chopped basil*	*10 ml*

Preheat oven to 450°F/230°C.

Make slits in the lamb and insert slivers of garlic. Place in a roaster, fat side up, and cover with onion slices. Sprinkle with lemon juice. Place in oven, reduce heat to 350°F/180°C and cook one hour, basting occasionally. Place potatoes around lamb and cook approximately one hour longer, or until potatoes are tender and lamb is done (about 170°F/77°C on a meat thermometer). Sprinkle basil over potatoes and serve on a platter with carved lamb.

Pele Sipi
TONGA

Serves 6

A tasty lamb main dish.

6	*lamb chops or mutton flaps*	*6*
1 tbsp	*butter*	*15 ml*
1	*large onion, sliced*	*1*
1 cup	*water*	*250 ml*
¼ tsp	*salt*	*1 ml*
1	*bunch pele leaves, or 1 medium bokchoy*	*1*

Place meat and butter in skillet and brown on both sides for 5 to 10 minutes.

Set meat aside and gently fry onion in remaining fat. Pour off excess fat, return meat to pan along with water and salt and simmer, covered, about 30 minutes or until tender.

Slice pele or bokchoy leaves and add to skillet, cooking for 5 to 7 minutes longer.

Mansaf
JORDAN

Serves 4

This traditional Jordanian dish of rich lamb, spicy rice and tangy yogurt sauce is easy to prepare and deliciously different.

4	*lamb shoulder chops*	*4*
1 tbsp	*butter*	*15 ml*
1	*medium onion, sliced and separated into rings*	*1*
½ cup	*water*	*125 ml*
3 in	*cinnamon stick*	*7.5 cm*
1¾ cups	*water*	*450 ml*
¾ cup	*long grain rice*	*200 ml*
¼ cup	*raisins*	*50 ml*
½ tsp	*salt*	*2 ml*
¼ tsp	*allspice*	*1 ml*
¼ tsp	*pepper*	*1 ml*
¼ tsp	*turmeric*	*1 ml*
½ cup	*plain yogurt*	*125 ml*
2 tbsp	*cream*	*30 ml*
2 tbsp	*parsley, chopped*	*30 ml*
1 tbsp	*flour*	*15 ml*
¼ cup	*slivered almonds*	*50 ml*

Season chops with salt and pepper. In large skillet brown lamb in butter. Remove, reserve fat. Add onion rings to fat and cook until transparent. Return lamb to pan, add ½ cup/125 ml water and cinnamon stick. Bring to boil, cover and simmer gently for 40 minutes.

Meanwhile in saucepan combine 1¾ cups/450 ml water and next six ingredients. Cover and simmer gently about 20 minutes or until rice is tender and all liquid absorbed.

For sauce, in separate pan combine yogurt, cream, parsley and flour. Cook until thick and bubbly, then simmer for 3 minutes, stirring constantly.

To serve, drain lamb mixture and discard cinnamon stick. Arrange lamb on serving platter. Stir nuts into rice mixture and arrange around lamb. Pour sauce on top, and serve remaining sauce separately.

Lamb Curry
INDIA

Serves 8

Beef, chicken or hard boiled eggs may be substituted for the lamb in this traditional curry.

2½ lbs	*lamb, cut in pieces*	*1.2 kg*
	vegetable oil or clarified butter	
3	*onions, finely chopped*	*3*
8	*cloves garlic, crushed*	*8*
3	*green peppers, chopped*	*3*
12	*hot green chilies (fresh)*	*12*
⅓ cup	*garam-masala (see below)*	*75 ml*
1¼ in	*piece ginger root*	*3 cm*
⅓ cup	*chili powder*	*75 ml*
1 tbsp	*salt*	*15 ml*
8	*medium tomatoes, chopped*	*8*
½ cup	*plain yogurt*	*125 ml*
2 tbsp	*fresh coriander or cilantro*	*30 ml*
2 cups	*water*	*500 ml*
2 lbs	*potatoes, quartered*	*1 kg*
3 tbsp	*lemon juice*	*45 ml*

In a large skillet brown lamb on all sides in oil or clarified butter and set aside. Fry onions, garlic, green peppers and chilies until golden, then push aside in pan. Add spices and fry for 2 more minutes. Add tomatoes, yogurt, parsley, browned meat and water. Cover and simmer on low heat for 1½ hours, stirring occasionally. Add potato pieces, and other vegetables if desired, and simmer a further 45 minutes. Add lemon juice 5 minutes before serving.

This curry may also be cooked in a Dutch oven at 300°F/160°C for 3 to 4 hours.

Note: Garam-masala may be made at home by grinding the following together in a blender:

1 tbsp	*black peppercorns*	*15 ml*
1 tbsp	*coriander seeds*	*15 ml*
1½ tsp	*caraway seeds*	*7 ml*
12	*cardamom pods (shelled)*	*12*
1 tbsp	*cloves*	*15 ml*
1 tbsp	*cinnamon*	*15 ml*

Paupiettes Lyonnaises

FRANCE

Serves 4

Paupiettes are popular throughout France, and have many variations. Serve on a bed of rice.

4	*veal escalopes*	*4*
1	*small egg yolk, beaten*	*1*
1	*clove garlic, crushed*	*1*
2 tbsp	*fresh parsley, chopped*	*30 ml*
1 tbsp	*fresh chives or green onions, chopped*	*15 ml*
1/8 tsp	*mace*	*pinch*
1/8 tsp	*nutmeg*	*pinch*
1/4 tsp	*salt*	*1 ml*
	freshly ground pepper	
4	*pork sausages*	*4*
4	*slices bacon*	*4*
4	*tomatoes, skinned*	*4*
1/4 cup	*butter, melted*	*50 ml*
4	*bay leaves*	*4*
	salt	
	pepper	
4	*sprigs fresh parsley*	*4*
4	*sprigs fresh thyme*	*4*

Preheat oven to 350°F/180°C.

Pound veal to flatten.

To make stuffing, combine egg yolk, garlic, parsley, chives, mace, nutmeg, salt and pepper; mix well. Remove raw sausage meat from its casing, and mix thoroughly with egg-herb mixture. Place a quarter of stuffing on each piece of veal and roll up to encase stuffing. Wrap a bacon slice around each escalope, making sure to cover exposed stuffing ends. Secure with toothpicks, or string tied "package style". Refrigerate 15 minutes, or up to several hours.

Remove tomato skins by dipping in boiling water, then into ice water. Arrange tomatoes and paupiettes in a generously greased, shallow casserole dish, and pour melted butter over all. Season generously with salt and pepper, and sprinkle with parsley and thyme.

Cover and bake for 1 hour, turning paupiettes twice to ensure even baking. Cook, uncovered, a further 10 minutes.

Serve on a bed of rice. If desired, pour pan juices over all.

Note: This dish can easily be increased to serve as many guests as desired.

Veal Escalope
AUSTRIA

Serves 6

It has been said that Austrians rank eating second only to music as a national pastime. This recipe is one of many outstanding Austrian dishes.

6	*veal cutlets*	*6*
½ cup	*flour*	*125 ml*
¾ tsp	*salt*	*3 ml*
¼ tsp	*pepper*	*1 ml*
⅓ cup	*butter*	*75 ml*
¼ cup	*water*	*50 ml*
1 tbsp	*capers, chopped*	*15 ml*
½ tsp	*paprika*	*2 ml*
1 tsp	*prepared mustard*	*5 ml*
2 tsp	*fresh lemon juice*	*10 ml*
1 tbsp	*cornstarch*	*15 ml*
1 cup	*whipping cream*	*250 ml*
6	*lemon wedges*	*6*
2 tbsp	*fresh parsley, chopped*	*30 ml*

Trim excess fat and connective membrane from cutlets. Pound cutlets to flatten and tenderize.

Combine flour, salt and pepper, and dredge cutlets. Melt butter in skillet on medium heat, add veal and fry cutlets until golden brown, about 3 minutes per side. Remove skillet from heat. Transfer cutlets to platter and keep warm.

Blend water, capers, paprika, mustard, lemon juice and cornstarch. Pour mixture into cooled skillet and blend with pan juices. Simmer 2 to 3 minutes, stirring constantly to scrape bottom of pan. Turn heat to low, add cream and blend thoroughly. Adjust seasonings. Heat sauce through until slightly thickened.

Pour sauce over veal and serve immediately, garnished with lemon wedges and fresh parsley.

Piccata al Limone

ITALY

Serves 6

A bonus for busy cooks: the flavour of this lemon-veal dish is enhanced if prepared in advance.

1 lb	*veal*	*500 g*
2 tbsp	*fresh lemon juice*	*30 ml*
½ cup	*flour*	*125 ml*
1 tsp	*salt*	*5 ml*
½ tsp	*pepper*	*2 ml*
½ cup	*butter*	*125 ml*
1	*large onion, sliced*	*1*
¾ cup	*white wine*	*200 ml*

Pound and flatten veal, trimming off fat. Sprinkle with lemon juice and set aside. Mix flour, salt and pepper and sprinkle over one side of the meat.

Melt butter in frying pan over medium heat and fry onion slices until soft. Remove onions; sauté veal 1 to 2 minutes per side or until just cooked. When veal has been sautéed, lay onions on top and pour on wine. Cover and simmer for 10 minutes.

Serve immediately garnished with sprigs of parsley.

Note: To prepare in advance, reduce final simmering time to 5 minutes. Place veal mixture in casserole and let cool completely before covering and freezing. To reheat, allow dish to come to room temperature, then cook, covered, for approximately 10 to 15 minutes at 350°F/180°C.

Swiss Cheese Fondue
SWITZERLAND

Serves 6

Cheese fondue, originally a speciality of the cantons of Western Switzerland, was traditionally served during the winter months. Today it is a year-round favourite in many parts of the world.

2	*cloves garlic, 1 finely chopped, 1 split in half*	2
7 oz	*dry white wine*	*225 ml*
½ lb	*Swiss Gruyère cheese, grated*	250 g
¼ lb	*Swiss Emmenthal cheese, grated*	*125 g*
⅛ tsp	*nutmeg*	*pinch*
⅛ tsp	*pepper, freshly ground*	*pinch*
2 tbsp	*Kirschwasser*	*30 ml*
1 tbsp	*cornstarch*	*15 ml*
2 tbsp	*water*	*30 ml*
1	*loaf french bread, cut in bite-sized cubes*	*1*

Thoroughly rub the inside of the earthenware fondue dish, known as a "caquelon" with the split garlic. Pour wine into fondue dish, and over medium heat bring to temperature of 160°F/70°C.

Mix cheese together and slowly add to wine, stirring in one direction only to prevent formation of lumps. Once blended, the fondue must be stirred continually until served. Add spices and finely chopped garlic. In a small cup mix together Kirschwasser, cornstarch and water and add to fondue. Increase heat, and continue stirring until fondue is smooth and bubbly.

When fondue is ready, place on preheated element at centre of dining table. Guests place a piece of bread on the end of a fork and dip it into the fondue. Everyone continues to stir the fondue to keep it well mixed.

Mushroom Crêpes

NETHERLANDS

Serves 4

For something quick and impressive, have frozen crêpes on hand to fill with our mushroom, wine and cheese recipe.

Crêpe Batter (makes 8):

1/2 cup	*flour*	*125 ml*
1/4 tsp	*salt*	*1 ml*
1/2 tsp	*baking powder*	*2 ml*
1	*large egg*	*1*
1 cup	*milk*	*250 ml*
	peanut oil	

Filling:

1/4 lb	*bacon, finely chopped*	*125 g*
1 tbsp	*butter*	*15 ml*
1	*onion, finely chopped*	*1*
1	*clove garlic, crushed*	*1*
1 lb	*fresh mushrooms, sliced*	*500 g*
1/3 cup	*red wine*	*75 ml*
1 tbsp	*flour*	*15 ml*
1 tbsp	*cream*	*15 ml*
1/4 tsp	*salt*	*1 ml*
1/8 tsp	*pepper*	*pinch*
1/8 tsp	*cayenne pepper*	*pinch*
1/2 cup	*Dutch Edam cheese, grated*	*125 ml*

To prepare crêpes: Sift together dry ingredients in a medium bowl. Beat egg and milk; make a well in dry ingredients and pour in egg mixture. Mix as little as possible; ignore small lumps, they will disappear.

Heat a 5 in/13 cm skillet or crêpe pan. Add a few drops of peanut oil. Pour in a small quantity of batter, tipping pan to allow batter to spread thinly over the bottom. Cook crêpe over medium heat until brown in patches on the bottom. Flip and brown other side. Repeat process until all batter is used up.

Note: To freeze crêpes, allow them to cool completely before stacking between layers of wax paper. Wrap in plastic wrap before freezing.

Filling: Preheat oven to 350°F/180°C.

Fry chopped bacon until partially cooked. Pour off excess fat. Add butter, stir in onion and garlic and fry until very light in colour. Lay mushrooms on top of onion mixture, add wine. Simmer 5 minutes or until done.

Combine flour and cream, add to mushroom mixture and stir to thicken. Add salt, pepper and cayenne to taste. Divide filling between 8 crêpes. Carefully roll up filled crêpes and lay in a lightly greased, flat ovenproof dish. Sprinkle with grated cheese and bake about 10 minutes until cheese is bubbling and mixture is heated through.

Place under broiler for a minute or two to brown the topping. Serve immediately. Suggested vegetables: fresh asparagus and tomato halves.

Accompaniments

Gages
SIERRA LEONE

Serves 6

This vegetable dish is a firm favourite with visitors to Sierra Leone.

1	*medium eggplant, skinned, sliced and lightly fried in butter or oil*	*1*
1	*medium hot pepper, finely chopped*	*1*
4	*medium tomatoes, sliced*	*4*
1	*medium red onion, sliced*	*1*
¼ cup	*vinegar*	*50 ml*
3 tbsp	*vegetable oil*	*45 ml*
¼ cup	*grated coconut*	*50 ml*
¼ cup	*unsalted peanuts*	*50 ml*

Prepare vegetables and place in large bowl. Combine vinegar and oil, pour over vegetables and toss gently. Chill for several hours.

Before serving, add coconut and peanuts.

Turkish Vegetable Mélange
TURKEY

Serves 6 to 8

Brief cooking time and olive oil are the secrets of this simple-to-prepare and versatile bean dish.

2 lbs	*fresh green beans, sliced*	*1 kg*
½ cup	*olive oil*	*125 ml*
4	*tomatoes, diced*	*4*
2	*small onions, diced*	*2*
2	*green peppers, diced*	*2*
1½ tsp	*salt*	*7 ml*
1 tsp	*black pepper*	*5 ml*
2 tsp	*sugar*	*10 ml*
1 cup	*water*	*250 ml*

Combine all ingredients in medium saucepan. Stir, cover and cook approximately 10 minutes until just tender. Serve hot or cold.

Broccoli Casserole

UNITED STATES OF AMERICA

Serves 6 to 8

This tasty broccoli-cheese dish is simple to make and freezes well.

2	*10 oz packages frozen broccoli or*	*566g*
1½ lb	*fresh broccoli, chopped*	*750 g*
2 tbsp	*melted butter*	*30 ml*
2 tbsp	*flour*	*30 ml*
¼ tsp	*salt*	*1 ml*
⅛ tsp	*dry mustard*	*pinch*
⅛ tsp	*pepper*	*pinch*
1 cup	*milk*	*250 ml*
½ cup	*mayonnaise*	*125 ml*
1 tbsp	*onion or chives, finely chopped*	*15 ml*
3	*eggs, well beaten*	*3*
1 cup	*cheddar cheese, grated*	*250 ml*

Preheat oven to 350°F/180°C.

Cook frozen broccoli according to package directions, or boil chopped fresh broccoli for about 10 minutes until crisp and tender.

In another pan, blend butter, flour, salt, mustard and pepper and cook until bubbly. Gradually stir in milk and cook until thickened. Remove from heat and stir in mayonnaise, onion, eggs and cheese. Mix with broccoli and pour into a greased casserole. Set in a pan of hot water and bake, uncovered, for 30 minutes.

Northern Vegetables

NORTHWEST TERRITORIES

Serves 6

You don't have to live in the far north, where fresh produce is often scarce, to enjoy this "casserole from a can".

2	*14 oz cans green beans*	*796 ml*
1	*10 oz condensed cream of mushroom soup*	*284 ml*
¼ cup	*flaked almonds or breadcrumbs*	*50 ml*
4 tsp	*butter*	*20 ml*

Preheat oven to 350°F/180°C.

Drain beans. Place in greased 2 qt/2 l casserole. Mix undiluted soup into beans. Top with almonds or breadcrumbs and dot with butter. Bake, uncovered, for 20 minutes.

Green Beans Supreme
AUSTRALIA

Serves 6

Fresh green beans with golden crunchy almonds - delicious!

1¼ lbs	*fresh green beans*	*750 g*
2 tbsp	*butter*	*30 ml*
2 tbsp	*fresh lemon juice*	*30 ml*
2 tbsp	*fresh parsley, chopped*	*30 ml*
	salt and pepper to taste	
2 tbsp	*slivered almonds, toasted*	*30 ml*

Top, tail and string beans. Cook in boiling, salted water for 10 minutes or until tender. Drain thoroughly. Melt butter in saucepan, add lemon juice and parsley. Stir until combined, add beans and heat through gently. Season with salt and pepper, and toss with almonds just before serving.
Note: For golden, crunchy almonds, add melted butter when toasting.

Goma Ae
JAPAN

Serves 6 to 8

Green beans with sesame seeds and soy sauce make a tasty dish.

1 lb	*green beans*	*500 g*
¼ cup	*sesame seeds*	*50 ml*
¼ cup	*soy sauce*	*50 ml*
2 tbsp	*sugar*	*30 ml*

Cut tips off the beans and remove the stringy fibre. Cook beans in boiling salted water about 10 minutes or until just tender. Rinse quickly in cold water to stop further cooking, and drain well. Keep warm in oven.

Heat sesame seeds in ungreased skillet over low to medium heat until they begin to jump, stirring constantly and watching for signs of burning. Crush toasted seeds between sheets of wax paper with a rolling pin.

Mix seeds with soy sauce and sugar and toss into warm beans. Serve immediately.

Carrots in White Wine
AUSTRIA

Serves 6

A tasty way to dress up carrots.

2 lbs	*carrots, peeled and cut into coins*	*1 kg*
1½ cups	*celery, diced*	*375 ml*
½ cup	*onion, chopped*	*125 ml*
¾ cup	*dry white wine*	*200 ml*
¼ cup	*sugar*	*50 ml*
¼ cup	*butter*	*50 ml*
1 tsp	*dill weed*	*5 ml*
¼ tsp	*salt*	*1 ml*
⅛ tsp	*pepper*	*pinch*

In a large saucepan combine above ingredients. Stir to blend. Cover and cook over low heat for approximately 15 minutes or until carrots are tender. Do not overcook. Adjust seasonings.

Cucumber Raita
INDIA

Serves 8

A cool accompaniment to curries and other meats, cooked potatoes or raw zucchini could be used instead of cucumbers.

2	*cucumbers, sliced or chopped*	2
1 cup	*sour cream*	*250 ml*
1½ tsp	*caraway seeds*	*7 ml*
1 tsp	*garam-masala (see Lamb Curry)*	*5 ml*
1 tsp	*chili powder*	*5 ml*
1½ tsp	*salt*	*7 ml*
½ tsp	*black pepper*	*2 ml*

Slice cucumbers very thin. Beat sour cream and add spices. Carefully fold in cucumber slices.

Refrigerate for 3 to 4 hours before using, to allow the sour cream to become infused with the spices.

Zatziki
GREECE

Serves 6

Zatziki, a cucumber salad, is traditionally served in small, individual bowls as an accompaniment to roast lamb.

1	*medium cucumber*	*1*
2 cups	*plain yoghurt*	*500 ml*
½ cup	*olive oil*	*125 ml*
3	*cloves garlic, crushed*	*3*
	salt and pepper to taste	
½ tsp	*dried mint*	*2 ml*

Peel cucumber and chop into small pieces. Mix next five ingredients. Add cucumber and stir gently. Refrigerate at least an hour before serving.

Stuffed Christophene
TRINIDAD

Serves 4

Christophene, or chayote squash, is mild tasting and makes an easy and attractive vegetable dish.

2	*christophenes*	*2*
1	*medium onion, chopped*	*1*
¼ cup	*butter*	*50 ml*
⅓ cup	*cheddar cheese, grated*	*75 ml*
¼ tsp	*salt*	*1 ml*
⅛ tsp	*pepper*	*pinch*
1 tbsp	*butter*	*15 ml*

Cut christophenes in half lengthwise. Cook in boiling, salted water for about 30 minutes until tender, not soft. Drain, discard seeds, and scoop out flesh leaving shells about ¼ in/.65 cm thick. Chop flesh coarsely, set aside.

Preheat oven to 350°F/180°C.

Sauté onions in butter for about 5 minutes or until transparent. Add chopped christophene, ¾ of the cheese, salt and pepper. Cook, stirring, until cheese is melted and mixture is well blended. Fill christophene shells with hot mixture, dot with butter and sprinkle with remaining cheese. Bake for 20 minutes or until tops are golden.

Gut Kuri Kimchi
SOUTH KOREA

Serves 6 to 8

This pickled cabbage is a must at all Korean meals!

1	*Chinese cabbage*	*1*
2	*cloves garlic, crushed*	*2*
1 tsp	*hot pepper sauce*	*5 ml*
1 tbsp	*soy sauce*	*15 ml*
1 tsp	*vinegar*	*5 ml*
1 tbsp	*salt*	*15 ml*
1 tbsp	*sugar*	*15 ml*

Shred cabbage; 6 cups are needed.

Blend garlic with hot pepper, soy sauce and vinegar. Add cabbage and mix well. Add salt and sugar and mix. Cover, and refrigerate at least 1 - 2 days.

Sweet and Sour Red Cabbage
SWEDEN

Serves 6 to 8

This superb vegetable dish is even better if made a day ahead and then reheated.

3 lbs	*red cabbage*	*1.5 kg*
¼ cup	*butter*	*50 ml*
1 tbsp	*sugar*	*15 ml*
2 tbsp	*apple cider vinegar*	*30 ml*
½ cup	*water*	*125 ml*
½ cup	*red currant jelly*	*125 ml*
1	*large apple, cored and grated*	*1*
	salt and pepper to taste	

Preheat oven to 325°F/165°C.

Slice cabbage finely after removing tough outer leaves and core.

In heavy Dutch oven (not aluminum), heat butter and melt sugar without browning. Add cabbage and cook for 5 minutes, stir in vinegar and water. Cover and bake for 2 to 3 hours or until very tender, adding more water as needed. Alternatively, simmer on stove top for same length of time.

Add red currant jelly, grated apple, salt and pepper 15 minutes before cabbage is done. Gently mix to blend.

Eggplant Relleno
PHILLIPINES

Serves 6

Buy eggplant that has a glossy colour, firm taut skin, and flesh that bounces back when lightly pressed.

3	*large eggplants*	*3*
	salt	
	olive oil	
	water	
4	*cloves garlic, crushed*	*4*
2	*small onions, chopped*	*2*
4	*medium tomatoes, chopped*	*4*
1 lb	*ground pork*	*500 g*
1 tsp	*salt*	*5 ml*
¼ tsp	*pepper*	*1 ml*
2	*eggs, beaten*	*2*
½ cup	*breadcrumbs*	*125 ml*

Halve unpeeled eggplant lengthwise and cross-cut exposed flesh. Sprinkle with salt and drain, flesh side down, for at least 30 minutes. (A weight placed on eggplant will speed up time.) Squeeze and pat dry.

Preheat oven to 425°F/215°C.

Run knife around eggplant skin ½ in/1.3 cm in from edge. Brush with oil. Add a little water to cover bottom of baking pan, place eggplant halves, skin side down and bake for 15 to 20 minutes or until tender. Loosen flesh with knife, scoop out, and chop. Set aside.

While eggplant is cooking, sauté garlic, onions, tomatoes and ground pork until meat is no longer pink. Season with salt and pepper. Drain off excess fat if necessary. Add chopped eggplant flesh.

Divide filling between eggplant halves. Brush tops with beaten egg and sprinkle generously with breadcrumbs. Return to pan and bake for approximately 8 minutes. Place under broiler for a minute or two to brown. Serve hot.

Fiddleheads with Bacon and Cheese Sauce

NEW BRUNSWICK

Serves 6

Fiddleheads are tedious to clean, but sweet to eat, and the flavour is a mixture of spinach and asparagus.

Sauce:

¼ cup	*butter or margarine*	*50 ml*
¼ cup	*flour*	*50 ml*
2 cups	*milk*	*500 ml*
1 cup	*mild cheddar cheese, grated*	*250 ml*
½ tsp	*salt*	*2 ml*
⅛ tsp	*pepper*	*pinch*

Melt butter in saucepan, stir in flour and cook over low heat, stirring, for 2 minutes. Gradually add milk, stirring constantly. Continue to stir and cook over medium heat for about 3 minutes. Remove pan from heat and stir in cheese, salt and pepper. Adjust seasonings. Set sauce aside, but keep it warm.

8	*slices bacon, cooked and crumbled*	*8*
5 cups	*fresh fiddleheads*	*1.2l*
	or	
2	*10 oz packages frozen fiddleheads*	*566g*
2 tsp	*fresh chives, chopped*	*10 ml*

Cook bacon until crisp and drain on paper towels before crumbling. Set aside.

To cook fresh fiddleheads: clean and wash thoroughly 3 or 4 times. Drain, and in water which clings to them cook in covered saucepan for 5 to 10 minutes over low heat until just tender. Young ones cook in about 5 minutes, so keep a close check. Drain if necessary and place in a warmed serving dish. Pour cheese sauce over top and sprinkle with bacon and chives.

Piquant Peas
ONTARIO

Serves 6

A slightly different way to prepare frozen peas.

1	*12 oz package frozen peas*	*340 g*
¾ cup	*liquid from cooking the peas*	*175 ml*
2 tbsp	*butter*	*30 ml*
4	*green onions, sliced*	*4*
2 tsp	*flour*	*10 ml*
½ tsp	*salt*	*2 ml*
1 tsp	*sugar*	*5 ml*
⅛ tsp	*pepper*	*pinch*
¼ tsp	*nutmeg*	*1 ml*

Cook frozen peas according to package instructions, increasing water sufficiently to yield ¾ cup/175 ml cooking liquid. Drain and reserve liquid.

Sauté onions in melted butter. Stir in flour, salt, sugar and nutmeg. Add reserved liquid and cook over medium heat, stirring constantly until mixture is slightly thickened. Add peas and blend.

Note: If not serving immediately, keep over hot water in double boiler until ready to serve.

Cheesey Potatoes
ALBERTA

Serves 6

Here is a super potato casserole for meat, poultry or fish.

3	*large baking potatoes, peeled*	*3*
	salt	
	black pepper, coarsely ground	
4	*slices bacon, crisp-cooked*	*4*
1	*large onion, sliced*	*1*
2 cups	*sharp cheese, cubed*	*500 ml*
½ cup	*butter or margarine, cut into small pieces*	*125 ml*

Preheat oven to 350°F/180°C.

Slice potatoes into a 1½ qt/1.5 l casserole dish. Sprinkle with salt and pepper. Crumble bacon over potatoes. Add onion and cheese cubes. Dot evenly with butter. Cover and bake for 1 hour.

Glazed Sweet Potatoes and Bacon

BOTSWANA

Serves 6

An excellent accompaniment for baked ham.

4	*sweet potatoes*	*4*
1/4 cup	*butter*	*50 ml*
1/4 cup	*marmalade or apricot jam*	*50 ml*
4	*slices bacon, crisp cooked and crumbled*	*4*

Boil sweet potatoes in their jackets about 25 minutes or until tender. Peel and cut into cubes. In a frying pan melt butter and jam over low heat. Add sweet potatoes and turn in sauce until glazed and heated through.

Serve immediately with crumbled bacon as a garnish.

Potato Lefsa

NORWAY

Makes 12

This Norwegian pancake is an easy, tasty way to use leftover potatoes.

2 cups	*cooked, mashed potatoes*	*500 ml*
2 tbsp	*milk*	*30 ml*
1 tbsp	*melted butter*	*15 ml*
1/4 tsp	*salt*	*1 ml*
3/4 cup	*flour*	*200 ml*
	vegetable oil	

In a large bowl mix together potatoes, milk, butter and salt. Blend in flour. Knead briefly on a lightly floured board, adding extra flour to make a non-sticky dough. Divide dough into 12 equal balls. Roll each on a lightly floured board in 7 in/18 cm circles.

Lightly oil a heavy skillet and set over medium heat. Cook lefsa about 1 minute on each side, or until lightly browned.

Serve hot with meat, fish or poultry.

Note: Lefsa freezes well. To reheat, place in a 300°F/160°C oven for 20 minutes.

Lefsa may be served with a meat or other savoury fillings. Place a spoonful of filling mixture onto cooked lefsa circles, then roll up and slice.

Jansson's Temptation
SWEDEN

Serves 6 to 8

A rich, creamy potato dish, flavored with anchovy.

8	*medium potatoes*	*8*
3	*2 oz cans anchovy fillets, preferably packed in brine, not oil*	*170 g*
2	*medium onions, thinly sliced*	*2*
1/8 tsp	*white pepper*	*pinch*
2 cups	*whipping cream*	*500 ml*
2 tbsp	*breadcrumbs*	*30 ml*
1 tbsp	*butter*	*15 ml*

Preheat oven to 350°F/180°C.

Peel potatoes and cut into 2 in/5 cm shoestring strips. Drain anchovies. Save brine to use later.

Butter a 2 qt/2 l shallow casserole. Alternate layers of potato, onion, anchovies and a sprinkling of pepper, ending with a layer of potatoes.

Mix anchovy brine with cream and heat to simmering point. Pour over potatoes. Sprinkle with breadcrumbs and dot with butter.

Bake for 1½ hours, or until potatoes are soft and liquid is nearly absorbed. If top becomes too brown, cover loosely with foil during baking.

Fan Potatoes
AUSTRALIA

Serves 6

An attractive alternative to roast potatoes.

6	*medium potatoes*	*6*
2 tbsp	*butter, softened or melted*	*30 ml*
	parmesan cheese	

Preheat oven to 350°F/180°C.

Peel potatoes. Cut in half lengthwise. Place in buttered baking dish, cut side down. From the top, cut lengthwise again in 3/8 in/8 mm slices, taking care not to slice all the way through to the bottom. Generously brush with butter and sprinkle with parmesan.

Cover and bake for 1 hour. Uncover for last 5 minutes. Potatoes will be golden brown, and the slices will have fanned out.

Rutabaga Casserole
FINLAND

Serves 6

The flavour of this dish improves if prepared ahead of time and reheated.

1	*large rutabaga, peeled and cubed*	1
	water	
1 tsp	*salt*	*5 ml*
½ cup	*cream*	*125 ml*
¼ cup	*fine breadcrumbs*	*50 ml*
2	*eggs*	2
2 tsp	*sugar*	*10 ml*
¼ tsp	*nutmeg*	*1 ml*
	rutabaga cooking broth	
2 tbsp	*butter*	*30 ml*

Cook rutabaga in lightly salted water for approximately 20 minutes or until soft.

In small bowl soak breadcrumbs in cream.

When rutabaga is done, drain off cooking broth and set aside. Mash rutabaga or put it through a food processor. Beat eggs with a fork and add to rutabaga along with sugar, nutmeg, softened breadcrumbs, and a small amount of broth if mixture appears too thick.

Grease an ovenproof casserole and pour in mixture. Let cool, then cover with plastic wrap and refrigerate for up to 48 hours.

To cook, dot top of casserole with butter and bake, uncovered, in a 325°F/175°C oven for approximately 45 minutes.

Ufi Haka
TONGA

Serves 6

Yams cooked in coconut cream are really worth trying!

2	*medium yams*	2
½ cup	*coconut cream, fresh or canned*	*125 ml*
1½ cups	*water*	*375 ml*

Peel yams and cut into chunks. Bring coconut cream and water to a boil, add yams and simmer, covered, for about 30 minutes or until tender.

Note: Any type of root vegetable can be substituted for yams.

Baked Tomatoes
AUSTRALIA

Serves 6

Attractive and so easy!

3	*medium tomatoes*	*3*
2 tbsp	*butter*	*30 ml*
	salt and pepper	
2 tbsp	*fresh parsley, chopped*	*30 ml*
2	*green onions, chopped*	*2*

Preheat oven to 350°F/180°C.

Cut tomatoes in half, placed in greased, ovenproof dish. Dot each tomato with butter; sprinkle with salt and pepper. Bake, uncovered, for 10 minutes.

To serve, arrange on platter and sprinkle with mixture of parsley and onions.

Dilled Zucchini
HUNGARY

Serves 6

Make at the last minute and serve immediately.

4	*medium zucchini, sliced*	*4*
1	*clove garlic, crushed*	*1*
2 tbsp	*butter*	*30 ml*
½ tsp	*salt*	*2 ml*
⅛ tsp	*pepper*	*pinch*
1 tsp	*dillweed*	*5 ml*

Sauté zucchini and garlic in melted butter 6 to 8 minutes or until just golden. Sprinkle with salt, pepper and dillweed.

Sweet Fried and Crisp Noodles

THAILAND

Serves 8

An unusual blend of flavours and textures.

Sauce:

1 tbsp	*instant tamarind (from specialty shops)*	*15 ml*
½ cup	*boiling water*	*125 ml*
½ cup	*brown sugar*	*125 ml*
2 tbsp	*Nam Pla fish sauce*	*30 ml*
1 tsp	*cayenne pepper*	*5 ml*

Make sauce by dissolving tamarind in ½ cup/125 ml boiling water, together with sugar, Nam Pla and cayenne pepper. Set aside.

	peanut oil for frying	
½ lb	*Thai or Chinese rice noodles (Sen Mee or Py Mei Fun)*	*250 g*
1½ cups	*bean sprouts*	*375 ml*
¼ cup	*peanut oil*	*50 ml*
6 oz	*ground pork*	*185 g*
6 oz	*shrimps*	*185 g*
½ cup	*green or white onion, chopped*	*125 ml*
6	*cloves garlic, crushed*	*6*
1	*tofu cake, finely chopped*	*1*
2 tbsp	*yellow bean sauce*	*30 ml*
2 tbsp	*Nam Pla fish sauce*	*30 ml*
1 tbsp	*white vinegar*	*15 ml*
2 tbsp	*lemon or lime juice*	*30 ml*
2 tsp	*grated lemon or lime peel*	*10 ml*
1 tsp	*salt*	*5 ml*

Garnish:

½ cup	*green onions, finely sliced*	*125 ml*
½ cup	*Chinese parsley or fresh coriander*	*125 ml*
1	*large red hot pepper, very thinly sliced*	*1*
2	*limes, cut in wedges*	*2*
2	*red and green chili peppers, cut to form tulip-like flowers*	*2*

To fry noodles, heat 4 in/10 cm peanut oil to 400°F/200°C (smoking hot) and fry small handfuls of noodles for about 5 seconds until they puff up and float to top. Remove with slotted spoon and drain on paper towels. When drained, break up with your hands into a large salad bowl, add bean sprouts, and set aside.

In wok or skillet, heat peanut oil until smoking hot. Brown pork for 2 minutes, add shrimp, stirring, then onion and garlic. Stir fry another 20 seconds. Add bean curd, yellow bean sauce, Nam Pla, vinegar and lemon juice. Then add prepared tamarind sauce, grated lemon peel and salt. Bring to boil, reduce heat and simmer about 10 minutes until mixture thickens slightly. Allow to cool for 5 minutes. Just before serving pour mixture over noodles and bean sprouts and toss to coat.

Transfer noodles to large platter. Decorate with garnish. Add pepper "flowers" at the ends of platter.

Buttered Noodles

AUSTRIA

Serves 6

Serve as a substitute for potatoes or rice.

2 cups	*egg noodles*	*500 ml*
8 cups	*water*	*2 l*
2 tsp	*salt*	*10 ml*
1 tbsp	*vegetable oil*	*15 ml*
½ cup	*butter*	*125 ml*
⅛ tsp	*mace*	*pinch*
⅛ tsp	*black pepper*	*pinch*

Cook noodles in boiling, salted water to which 1 tbsp/15 ml oil has been added, for 6 to 8 minutes. Do not overcook. Drain.

Place butter in a heatproof casserole and add drained noodles. Sprinkle with mace and pepper. Reheat, tossing until noodles are coated with butter. Serve immediately.

Perogies

MANITOBA

Serves 6

Our testers found this recipe easy to prepare. It freezes well, and is an excellent meatless dinner.

Dough:

¾ cup	*milk*	*200 ml*
2 tbsp	*butter*	*30 ml*
1	*egg, well beaten*	*1*
2½ cups	*flour*	*625 ml*
½ tsp	*salt*	*2 ml*

Scald milk, remove from heat and add butter. Let cool slightly. Add egg and mix well. Combine flour and salt before adding to egg mixture. Knead dough on a lightly floured board until it is smooth and elastic. Roll out until approximately ¼ in/.65 cm thick and cut into 2 to 3 in/5 to 7.5 cm rounds. Roll each piece to a thickness of ⅛ in/.33 cm. Cover and set aside.

Filling:

4	*medium potatoes, peeled*	*4*
1 tsp	*onion salt*	*5 ml*
1 cup	*grated cheddar cheese*	*250 ml*
1 cup	*dry cottage cheese*	*250 ml*

Garnish:

butter
salt
sour cream

Boil potatoes. Drain, mash and add onion salt and cheeses. Mix well. Allow to cool. Hold circle of dough in palm of hand and place a rounded teaspoonful/5 ml of filling in centre. Fold in half and press moistened edges together. Lay on a flat dry surface and cover. Drop into boiling water and boil steadily for 4 to 5 minutes, or until perogies rise to the surface. Drain thoroughly before sprinkling with butter and salt. Serve hot with sour cream.

Perogies keep well in the refrigerator and can be reheated in boiling water, or sautéed in a little butter until golden brown.

Dumplings
HUNGARY

Serves 6

Meat, poultry or sauerkraut are delicious with these dumplings.

3	*eggs*	*3*
½ cup	*water*	*125 ml*
2 cups	*flour*	*500 ml*
1 tsp	*salt*	*5 ml*
1 tbsp	*butter*	*15 ml*

Thoroughly mix eggs and water, stir in flour and salt. Drop dough by teaspoonful/5 ml into 2 qt/2 l boiling, salted water. Cook, uncovered, for 10 minutes.Stir occasionally to prevent dumplings sticking together. Remove with slotted spoon. Toss with butter and serve immediately.

Rice with Peas
INDIA

Serves 8

This spicy rice dish is good with curry.

3 cups	*Basumati long grain Indian rice, or other long grain rice*	*750 ml*
¾ cup	*butter, oil or ghee*	*200 ml*
1 cup	*onions, finely chopped*	*250 ml*
6	*cloves*	*6*
3	*1 in/2.5 cm pieces cinnamon stick*	*3*
6 cups	*boiling water*	*1.5 l*
1½ tsp	*salt*	*7 ml*
1½ tsp	*turmeric*	*7 ml*
1	*10 oz package frozen peas*	*283 g*

If using Basumati rice, wash several times.

In the butter, gently fry onions, cloves and cinnamon pieces for 5 minutes. Add rice and cook a few minutes until golden brown. Add boiling water, salt, turmeric and peas and bring to a boil. Reduce heat, cover, and simmer for 20 minutes or until all water is absorbed and rice is soft.

Fried Rice
CHINA

Serves 6

Traditionally a side dish, by adding more meat and peas this becomes a complete meal.

3 cups	*salted water*	*750 ml*
1½ cups	*long grain rice*	*375 ml*
¼ cup	*peanut oil*	*50 ml*
2	*eggs, lightly beaten*	*2*
½ cup	*cooked ham, diced*	*125 ml*
½ cup	*shrimp meat, cooked*	*125 ml*
½ cup	*frozen peas*	*125 ml*
2	*green onions, thinly sliced*	*2*
1 tsp	*light soy sauce*	*5 ml*
¼ tsp	*five-spice*	*1 ml*
3 tbsp	*chicken stock*	*45 ml*

Bring salted water to boil and add rice. Cover and simmer gently for 20 minutes or until liquid is absorbed. Cool and chill.

Heat oil in pan to smoking point. Add eggs, stirring rapidly until set. Add rice and cook a further 2 to 3 minutes.

Lower to medium heat and add remaining ingredients. Stir fry about 5 minutes until thoroughly heated.

Haitian Rice

HAITI

Serves 6

This one pot dish is a Sunday favourite with Haitians, especially when shared at midday with friends and relatives.

¼ lb	*bacon*	*125 g*
1	*green pepper, coarsely chopped*	*1*
2	*cloves garlic, crushed*	*2*
1 lb	*shrimp*	*500 g*
1 cup	*long grain rice, uncooked*	*250 ml*
1	*14 oz can lima or kidney beans, drained*	*398 ml*
2 cups	*liquid (juice from beans plus water)*	*500 ml*
1 tsp	*salt*	*5 ml*
¼ tsp	*pepper*	*1 ml*
¼ tsp	*thyme*	*1 ml*
2 tbsp	*butter*	*30 ml*
2 tbsp	*parsley, chopped*	*30*
1	*lime, cut in wedges*	*1*

In a large frying pan cook bacon until crisp. Drain off all but 1 tbsp bacon fat. Add green pepper, garlic and shrimp and stir fry for 5 minutes over low heat. Remove bacon, green pepper, garlic and shrimp, set aside. Add rice to frying pan, adding extra bacon fat if necessary, and cook, stirring constantly for 5 minutes.

Drain lima or kidney beans and set aside; measure liquid from beans and add enough water to make 2 cups/500 ml. Add salt, pepper, thyme and liquid to rice in frying pan and stir to blend. Bring mixture to boil, cover, and simmer gently for 25 minutes. Add bacon, green pepper, garlic, shrimp and beans, stir gently and heat through about 5 minutes. Add butter and parsley, tossing lightly.

Serve piping hot, garnished with fresh lime wedges.

Risotto Milanese

ITALY

Serves 6

A delicious saffron dish, which can be served with veal, spiced beef or chicken. It is important to use short-grain Arborio rice, which is available at specialty stores.

½ cup	*butter*	*125 ml*
1	*medium onion, chopped*	*1*
2	*cloves garlic, crushed*	*2*
2 cups	*Italian Arborio rice*	*500 ml*
2	*10 oz cans chicken broth*	*568 ml*
1 oz	*dried wild mushrooms (porcini)*	*28 g*
1 tsp	*salt*	*5 ml*
1½ cups	*water or white wine*	*375 ml*
⅛ tsp	*powdered saffron, soaked in 1 tbsp/15 ml hot water*	*pinch*
¼ cup	*fresh parmesan cheese, grated*	*50 ml*

In a large, heavy saucepan, melt butter and sauté onion and garlic until translucent. Add rice and stir until well-coated. Cook 5 minutes or until rice becomes transparent. Slowly add chicken broth, mushrooms and salt, stirring frequently to prevent sticking. Simmer for approximately 30 to 45 minutes, occasionally adding enough water or wine to keep rice creamy but not runny. Add saffron and stir to blend.

Serve immediately. Garnish with parmesan cheese.

Wild Rice Casserole

SASKATCHEWAN

Serves 6

Since wild rice quadruples in volume when cooked, a small amount goes a long way. Our wild rice casserole is a delightful version of a famous prairie dish.

¾ cup	*wild rice*	*200 ml*
1½ cups	*water*	*375 ml*
1 tsp	*salt*	*5 ml*
½ cup	*butter*	*125 ml*
1 cup	*white rice, uncooked*	*250 ml*
1 cup	*onion, finely chopped*	*250 ml*
2 cups	*celery, finely chopped*	*500 ml*
4 cups	*fresh mushrooms, sliced*	*1 l*
1 cup	*water*	*250 ml*
1	*10 oz can consommé*	284 ml
1 tsp	salt	5 ml
½ tsp	*pepper*	*2 ml*
½ cup	*fresh parsley, chopped*	*125 ml*

In a medium pan combine wild rice, water and salt. Bring to boil, uncovered, and simmer 25 minutes or until just tender. Drain and set aside.

Preheat oven to 325°F/165°C.

Melt butter in frying pan. Add white rice, onion and celery; sauté, stirring constantly, for 3 minutes. Remove rice mixture and set aside. Sauté mushrooms in remaining butter. Remove mushrooms and deglaze pan, using the 1 cup/250 ml water. Combine the water with the white rice mixture, wild rice, consommé, salt, pepper, mushrooms and fresh parsley in buttered 2 qt/2 l casserole. Adjust seasonings, cover and bake in oven for 1 hour or until all moisture is absorbed.

Dhal
INDIA

Serves 8

Nutritious dhal is a traditional accompaniment to curried dishes.

2½ cups	*red or yellow lentils*	*625 ml*
7½ cups	*water*	*1.9 l*
⅓ cup	*butter or ghee*	*75 ml*
2	*medium onions, chopped*	*2*
1 tbsp	*garam-masala (see Lamb Curry)*	*15 ml*
2 tsp	*turmeric*	*10 ml*
2 tsp	*chili powder*	*10 ml*
⅓ cup	*fresh coriander, cilantro or Chinese parsley*	*75 ml*
4 tsp	*salt*	*20 ml*
½ tsp	*pepper*	*2 ml*

Wash lentils well to remove all grit. Place in saucepan with water, bring to a boil, reduce heat and simmer for 30 minutes until lentils are tender.

Meanwhile, fry onions, garam-masala, turmeric and chili powder in butter until onions are transparent and golden. Add to lentils, together with coriander, salt and pepper, and simmer for a further 10 minutes. Dhal should not be too mushy.

Chapattis
INDIA

Serves 6 to 8

This unleavened bread is a traditional accompaniment to curry.

2½ cups	*wholewheat flour*	*625 ml*
1½ tsp	*salt*	*7 ml*
1 cup	*water*	*250 ml*
4 cups	*oil or ghee*	*1 l*

Mix flour, salt and water together. Knead thoroughly for 5 minutes. Cover and set aside for 1 to 2 hours, then re-knead. Make small balls and on a floured board roll out like a thin pancake.

Heat oil or ghee in frying pan to 400°F/200°C. Fry chapattis one at a time for several minutes until puffed up and lightly browned. Keep hot in a damp cloth, with wax paper between each chapatti.

Bannock
NORTHWEST TERRITORIES

Serves 6

A Canadian classic!

4 cups	*flour*	*1 l*
3 tbsp	*baking powder*	*45 ml*
1/2 tsp	*salt*	*2 ml*
1/4 cup	*powdered milk*	*50 ml*
1/4 cup	*lard or bacon fat*	*50 ml*
2 cups	*water (or less)*	*500 ml*

Preheat oven to 450°F/230°C.

In a large bowl, mix dry ingredients. Using a pastry blender or two knives, cut in fat, finely. Gradually stir in water using a fork or wooden spoon to make a soft, slightly sticky ball of dough. Turn dough out on a lightly floured surface and knead 8 to 10 times. Roll out or pat to a thickness of 1/2 in/1.3 cm and place on lightly greased cookie sheet. Bake for 15 to 20 minutes, or until golden brown.

Cut and serve hot with butter.

Newfoundland Biscuits
NEWFOUNDLAND

Makes 12 biscuits

"Scrunchions" or cooked salt pork bits give this biscuit its unique flavour.

1/2 cup	*salt pork bits, or finely diced bacon*	*125 ml*
1 3/4 cups	*flour + 1 tbsp*	*465 ml*
1 tbsp	*baking powder*	*15 ml*
1/4 tsp	*salt*	*1 ml*
2 tbsp	*butter*	*30 ml*
1/4 cup	*molasses*	*50 ml*
3/4 cup	*water*	*200 ml*

Preheat oven to 425°F/220°C.

Fry pork or bacon until crisp. Drain well on paper towels. Sift together flour, baking powder and salt. Cut in butter until mixture is crumbly. Stir in pork bits. Combine molasses and water and stir into mixture to make a soft dough. Turn dough onto a floured board, knead lightly, and roll out to 1/2 in/1.3 cm thickness. Cut into 3 in/7.5 cm rounds. Bake on an ungreased baking sheet for 12 to 15 minutes.

Serve hot with butter.

Nova Scotia Oat Cakes
NOVA SCOTIA

Makes 5 to 6 dozen

The secret of traditional oatcakes lies in the use of lard and bacon fat.

3 cups	*rolled oats*	*750 ml*
3 cups	*flour*	*750 ml*
1 cup	*sugar*	*250 ml*
2 tsp	*salt*	*10 ml*
1 tsp	*baking soda*	*5 ml*
1¼ cups	*lard*	*300 ml*
¼ cup	*bacon fat*	*50 ml*
¾ cup	*cold water*	*175 ml*

Preheat oven to 325°F/160°C.

Mix together dry ingredients. Cut in lard and bacon fat until mixture is crumbly. Add water and work dough into a ball. Separate dough into three sections. Roll out each section on a well-floured board, shaping into a rectangle ⅛ in/2.5 mm thick (slightly thicker than pastry). Using a knife, cut dough into diamond shapes. Bake on an ungreased baking sheet for 15 minutes, or until golden brown.

Note: This recipe can be halved. The finished product freezes well.

Cornbread Stuffing
UNITED STATES OF AMERICA

Makes 8 cups/2 l

Perfect with your Thanksgiving turkey!

8 cups	*cornbread crumbs*	*2 l*
1 cup	*onion, chopped*	*250 ml*
1 cup	*celery, chopped*	*250 ml*
1 cup	*butter, melted*	*250 ml*
1½ tsp	*salt*	*7 ml*
¼ tsp	*pepper*	*1 ml*
½ tsp	*poultry seasoning*	*2 ml*
½ tsp	*sage*	*2 ml*
⅓ cup	*chicken broth or milk*	*75 ml*

Set breadcrumbs out to dry overnight. Sauté onion and celery in melted butter. Combine all ingredients, using only enough broth to barely moisten the bread. Stuff turkey just before cooking.

Cranberry-Orange Relish

UNITED STATES OF AMERICA

Makes 2 cups/500 ml

The delicate flavour of honey gives added interest to this fruit relish.

1	*apple, quartered, unpeeled*	*1*
1	*orange, quartered, unpeeled*	*1*
¼ cup	*water*	*50 ml*
⅔ cup	*honey*	*175 ml*
2 cups	*cranberries, fresh or frozen*	*500 ml*

Discarding only pips and core, place apple, orange and water in a blender. Chop finely.

In a small saucepan combine blended fruits and honey. Add cranberries and bring mixture to a boil over medium heat, stirring constantly. Boil for 5 minutes. Remove from heat.

Serve hot or cold.

Cranberry-Orange Relish Muffins

UNITED STATES OF AMERICA

Makes 18

Use leftover cranberry-orange relish to make this tea-time treat, or use fresh cranberries.

2⅓ cups	*flour*	*575 ml*
2 tsp	*baking powder*	*10 ml*
1½ tsp	*cinnamon*	*7 ml*
½ tsp	*salt*	*2 ml*
1 tsp	*baking soda*	*5 ml*
½ cup	*butter*	*125 ml*
¾ cup	*sugar*	*200 ml*
1	*egg*	*1*
2 cups	*cranberry-orange relish*	*500 ml*

Preheat oven to 375°F/190°C.

Sift together first 5 ingredients and set aside. In a large bowl, cream butter, sugar and egg until light. Stir in cranberry-orange relish. Add dry ingredients. Combine, stirring as little as possible. Fill greased or lined muffin tins ¾ full. Bake for 25 minutes.

Wild Cranberry Sauce
NORTHWEST TERRITORIES

Makes 3 cups

Delightful flavour!

3 cups	*uncooked wild cranberries, fresh or frozen*	*750 ml*
½ cup	*water*	*125 ml*
2 cups	*sugar*	*500 ml*

Cook cranberries and water over medium heat for 10 minutes, or until berries become soft. Add sugar, stir to blend and bring to full boil. Boil gently for 2 to 3 minutes.

Allow sauce to cool completely before storing in refrigerator or freezer.

Plum Sauce
CHINA

Makes 1½ cups/375 ml

A spicy sauce to serve with all Chinese dishes.

1	*14 oz can plums*	*398 ml*
2 tsp	*cornstarch*	*10 ml*
2 tbsp	*vinegar*	*30 ml*
¼ tsp	*allspice*	*1 ml*
¼ tsp	*ginger*	*1 ml*
½ tsp	*dry mustard*	*2 ml*
1 tbsp	*sugar*	*15 ml*
1 tbsp	*soy sauce*	*15 ml*
1 tbsp	*hoi sin sauce*	*15 ml*
1 tsp	*sesame oil*	*5 ml*

Drain plums, reserving ½ cup/125 ml juice. In saucepan blend juice and cornstarch.

Pit plums and place in blender along with remaining ingredients. Blend until smooth. Add to juice mixture and bring to boil over medium heat, stirring constantly. Lower heat and simmer 5 minutes.

Cool and refrigerate.

Seasoning – West Indian Style
BARBADOS

Makes approximately ½ cup/125 ml

In Barbados this popular seasoning is used as a marinade or stuffing for fried flying fish, shark and pork.

1	*medium onion, minced*	*1*
3	*green onions, or chives, chopped*	*3*
3	*cloves garlic, crushed*	*3*
¼ tsp	*thyme or marjoram*	*1 ml*
½ tsp	*salt*	*2 ml*
¼ tsp	*cloves, powdered*	*1 ml*
2 tbsp	*fresh lime juice*	*30 ml*
	fish or pork for frying	

Mix all ingredients until well blended.

Score fish or pork, and press seasoning generously into incisions. Marinate at least 30 minutes before frying.

Desserts

Almond Tortoni

ITALY

Serves 8

Almond Tortoni are a snap to prepare and their flavour improves if made a few weeks in advance and stored in the freezer.

1	*egg white*	*1*
¼ cup	*icing sugar*	*50 ml*
1 cup	*whipping cream*	*250 ml*
1 tbsp	*sherry or Marsala*	*15 ml*
1 tsp	*almond extract*	*5 ml*
1 cup	*almond macaroon crumbs*	*250 ml*
½ cup	*ground almonds*	*125 ml*
6	*red maraschino cherries, chopped*	*6*
6	*green maraschino cherries, chopped*	*6*
¼ cup	*slivered almonds*	*50 ml*
4	*maraschino cherries, halved for garnish*	*4*

In a small bowl, beat egg white until it forms a soft peak; gradually beat in sugar and continue beating until white is thick and glossy. Set aside.

In a large bowl whip cream and carefully fold in sherry or Marsala, almond extract, macaroon crumbs, ground almonds, and chopped cherries. Gently fold egg white into cream mixture.

Spoon into 8 paper baking cups placed in medium size muffin tray. Sprinkle with slivered almonds. Cover muffin tray with clear plastic wrap and then aluminum foil. Freeze overnight.

To serve, let sit for 5 minutes and garnish with maraschino cherry halves.

Baked Apple Dumplings
NEW BRUNSWICK

Serves 8

Use your favourite tart apples to make this family style dessert. Serve with whipped cream or ice cream.

2 ½ cups	*flour*	*625 ml*
5 tsp	*baking powder*	*25 ml*
1 tsp	*salt*	*5 ml*
¼ cup	*shortening*	*50 ml*
¾ cup	*milk*	*200 ml*
5	*large tart apples, peeled and diced*	*5*
1 cup	*seedless raisins*	*250 ml*
1 cup	*brown sugar*	*250 ml*
¼ cup	*water*	*50 ml*

Preheat oven to 300°F/150°C.

Sift dry ingredients together and cut in shortening. Add milk and mix quickly. Roll on a floured board to ½ in/1.3 cm thickness and cut into 16 small biscuits. Roll each biscuit out thinner, into a square shape, and add a portion of apples and raisins. Bring corners of pastry together at the top. Moisten edges and pinch together to hold mixture in place. Then turn upside down and place in a greased baking dish. Make a small hole on top and add about one tablespoonful/15 ml of water to each dumpling. Bake for about 1 hour. Mix 1 cup/250 ml brown sugar and ¼ cup/50 ml water and pour into dumplings. Bake for another 10 minutes.

Note: Recipe can easily be cut in half.

Apple Nut Pudding
TURKEY

Serves 6

A quick, hearty dessert served warm with rich cream or ice cream.

4	*tart apples*	*4*
¼ cup	*fresh lemon juice*	*50 ml*
1 cup	*flour*	*250 ml*
3 tbsp	*brown sugar*	*45 ml*
1 tbsp	*chopped walnuts*	*15 ml*
2 tbsp	*slivered almonds*	*30 ml*
½ cup	*raisins*	*125 ml*
1 tsp	*baking powder*	*5 ml*
1	*egg, beaten*	*1*
1 tsp	*vanilla*	*5 ml*
2 tbsp	*water*	*30 ml*

Peel, core and coarsely chop apples and put in bowl. Toss with lemon juice.

Preheat oven to 350°F/180°C.

In medium bowl, mix flour, sugar, nuts, raisins, and baking powder. Stir in egg, vanilla, water, and apples. Add more water if mixture appears too dry.

Grease shallow 8 in/20 cm square baking pan and spoon in apple batter. Bake, uncovered for 30 minutes.

Allow pudding to cool slightly before serving with vanilla custard, rich cream or ice cream.

Date and Banana Dessert
JORDAN

Serves 6

This rich dessert couldn't be simpler.

6	*bananas, sliced*	*6*
½ lb	*dates, fresh or dried*	*250 g*
1	*grated peel from an orange*	*1*
1¼ cups	*light cream*	*300 ml*

Arrange alternate layers of bananas, dates, and a sprinkling of grated orange peel in an attractive serving bowl. Pour cream over all and chill for several hours (not overnight), before serving.

Irish Bananas

REPUBLIC OF IRELAND

Serves 4

Add a little "Irish spirit" to your dessert menu.

½ cup	*butter*	*125 ml*
½ cup	*golden sugar*	*125 ml*
½ cup	*Irish whiskey*	*125 ml*
4	*large bananas, peeled and halved lengthwise*	*4*

Melt butter in skillet over medium heat. Add sugar and whiskey. Bring to a boil and stir until sugar dissolves. Add bananas and simmer gently for 5 minutes or until bananas are tender and glazed with sugar mixture.

Serve bananas immediately, topped with ice cream.

P.E.I. Bread Pudding

PRINCE EDWARD ISLAND

Serves 4

An unusual approach to an economical, tasty dessert.

1 cup	*brown sugar, packed firmly*	*250 ml*
4	*slices bread, buttered*	*4*
2	*eggs*	*2*
2 cups	*milk*	*500 ml*
¼ tsp	*salt*	*1 ml*
1 tsp	*vanilla*	*5 ml*

Sprinkle brown sugar in the top of a double boiler. Lay 4 buttered slices of bread over the sugar. In a small bowl, whip eggs, milk, salt and vanilla. Pour this mixture over the bread. Cover and cook for 1½ hours in the double boiler. Keep water in bottom pan boiling gently and add more water as necessary.

Irish Autumn Pudding

REPUBLIC OF IRELAND

Serves 6 to 8

If blackberries are unavailable, substitute raspberries to make this traditional favourite. This dessert should be made a day ahead.

3/4 lb	*blackberries*	*375 g*
1 lb	*tart cooking apples, peeled, cored and sliced*	*500 g*
1 cup	*sugar*	*250 ml*
1/4 cup	*water*	*50 ml*
1 tbsp	*gelatine*	*10 g*
1/4 cup	*water*	*50 ml*
1/2	*loaf white bread, sliced, crusts removed*	*1/2*
	icing sugar, whipped cream or vanilla custard to garnish	

Cook apple slices, blackberries, sugar and 1/4 cup water for 20 to 30 minutes or until soft. Dissolve gelatine in remaining 1/4 cup water over medium heat, stirring to dissolve completely. Add gelatine to cooked fruit mixture.

Line a 1 1/2 qt/1.5 l greased pudding basin or mixing bowl with bread and pour in fruit mixture. Top with a layer of bread slices. Place a saucer, and a weight on top and refrigerate overnight.

Turn out onto a plate and decorate with icing sugar, whipped cream or vanilla custard.

Note: If using raspberries instead of blackberries, add a little cornstarch to thicken.

Blueberry Cobbler
NEWFOUNDLAND

Serves 6

Blueberries were known as "whortleberries" or "hurtleberries" to the early English settlers and today play a popular part in Canadian cookery.

Base:

3 cups	*blueberries, fresh or frozen*	*750 ml*
⅓ cup	*sugar*	*75 ml*
1 tbsp	*fresh lemon juice*	*15 ml*
2 tsp	*salt*	*10 ml*
2 tbsp	*butter, melted*	*30 ml*
½ tsp	*cinnamon*	*2 ml*

Combine above ingredients and spread over the bottom of a 9 x 13 in/22.5 x 32.5 cm oven-proof dish.

Dough:

1½ cups	*flour*	*375 ml*
2 tsp	*baking powder*	*10 ml*
½ tsp	*salt*	*2 ml*
¼ cup	*sugar*	*50 ml*
¼ tsp	*cloves, powdered*	*1 ml*
½ cup	*shortening*	*125 ml*
¾ cup	*milk*	*175 ml*

Preheat oven to 375°F/190°C.

Combine flour, baking powder, salt, sugar and cloves. Cut in shortening and mix in milk to form a soft dough. Drop by tablespoonfuls close together onto blueberry mixture. Bake in oven for 40 minutes. Serve warm, topped with whipped cream or custard.

Carrot Halva
INDIA

Serves 6 to 8

Serve this sweet, chilled dessert after a spicy meal.

9	*medium carrots, finely grated*	*9*
6 cups	*milk*	*1.5 l*
1 cup	*light cream*	*250 ml*
1 cup	*brown sugar*	*250 ml*
1 cup	*white sugar*	*250 ml*
½ cup	*molasses*	*125 ml*
2 cups	*almonds, ground*	*500 ml*
1 tsp	*cardamom seeds, finely ground*	*5 ml*
⅓ cup	*butter*	*75 ml*

In a large, heavy pan, put carrots, milk and cream. On medium heat bring to just below boiling, stirring constantly. Reduce heat and simmer for 1 hour until mixture thickens, stirring regularly to prevent sticking to pan. Add sugars and molasses and cook a further 30 minutes. Add ground almonds, cardamom and butter, and stir again on a very low heat until mixture thickens. Pour halva into a large square cake pan and smooth with a spatula. Cool and refrigerate.

Decorate halva with edible silver leaves or slivered nuts before slicing and serving.

Classique au Chocolat à l'Orange
FRANCE

Serves 6 to 10

A little of this exquisitely rich treat, which has a thin crust on the outside and a creamy mousse inside, will satisfy most dessert lovers.

4	*egg yolks*	*4*
1 cup	*berry sugar*	*250 ml*
1	*grated rind of a large orange*	*1*
7 oz	*semi-sweet chocolate*	*200 g*
3 tbsp	*strong coffee*	*45 ml*
⅔ cup	*butter, softened*	*175 ml*
1 tbsp	*flour plus 1 tsp*	*20 ml*
½ tsp	*corn starch*	*2 ml*
4	*egg whites*	*4*
⅛ tsp	*salt*	*pinch*

Preheat oven to 350°F/180°C.

Generously grease and flour a 9 in/23 cm springform pan. In a large bowl, using an electric mixer, beat egg yolks with sugar for 8 minutes. Add orange rind and blend thoroughly. Set aside.

In a small pot, melt chocolate and coffee over very low heat. Cool slightly, and stir to blend before adding to egg yolk mixture. Immediately add butter and stir with a wooden spoon. Add flour and corn starch, blend well. Set aside.

Using an electric mixer, whip egg whites and salt until stiff. Very gently fold egg whites into chocolate mixture. Pour into pan and bake for 35 minutes.

Let dessert sit for 5 minutes before removing from pan. Serve lukewarm.

Pot de Chocolat

ONTARIO

Serves 6

Exquisitely rich and a snap to prepare.

1 cup	*semi-sweet chocolate chips*	*250 ml*
1¼ cups	*scalded light cream*	*300 ml*
2	*egg yolks*	2
2 tbsp	*dark rum, orange flavoured liqueur, or brandy*	*30 ml*
	whipped cream, flaked chocolate or finely grated orange rind to garnish	

Combine first four ingredients in a blender. Process until smooth and creamy. Pour into demitasse cups. Chill for a minimum of 4 hours.

Garnish just before serving.

Cloudberry Parfait
FINLAND

Serves 6

Cloudberries are a raspberry-like wild fruit found in Northern Europe.

2	*egg yolks*	2
⅓ cup	*berry sugar*	*75 ml*
½ tsp	*vanilla*	*2 ml*
1 cup	*whipping cream*	*250 ml*
1 cup	*cloudberries or raspberries*	*250 ml*

In a medium bowl whip egg yolks, sugar and vanilla. Whip cream until thick and fold into egg yolk mixture. Purée berries and carefully fold into egg-cream mixture. Pour into shallow jelly mold or straightsided springform pan. Freeze at least 4 hours.

Unmold onto platter, decorate with extra whipped cream and whole berries. Cut in wedges to serve.

Magic Cream
NORWAY

Serves 6

Light, fluffy — a dessert low in calories. The name "magic cream" comes from the fact that the egg whites "grow" as they are whipped.

3	*egg whites*	*3*
3 tbsp	*sugar*	*45 ml*
½	*juice of ½ lemon*	½
1 cup	*applesauce*	*250 ml*
2 tbsp	*red jam or jelly*	*30 ml*

Beat egg whites until very stiff, add sugar and lemon juice. Whip to a fluffy cream. Carefully fold in the applesauce and the jam or jelly.

Spoon into small dessert dishes and serve immediately.

Diplomate
BELGIUM

Serves 6

Popular in Belgium and France, this dessert is best served at room temperature with a cup of rich, dark coffee.

16	*ladyfingers*	*16*
¼ cup	*apricot jam*	*50 ml*
⅔ cup	*light rum*	*175 ml*
2 tbsp	*very hot water*	*30 ml*
2 cups	*thin vanilla custard*	*500 ml*
⅛ tsp	*salt*	*pinch*
1 tsp	*vanilla*	*5 ml*
2 tbsp	*flaked almonds*	*30 ml*

To assemble dessert, spread apricot jam on half the ladyfingers. Top with remaining ladyfingers to make "sandwiches". In a medium bowl combine rum and water. Soak each ladyfinger sandwich in bowl for a moment. Line bottom and sides of an attractive serving bowl with ladyfingers. Pour remaining rum mixture over the "sandwiches".

Using your favourite recipe, prepare a thin vanilla custard, adding extra salt and vanilla as called for in this recipe. If using commercial custard mix, add twice as much milk as the instructions call for to achieve a thin custard. Allow custard to cool until barely warm before pouring over ladyfingers.

Decorate custard with flaked almonds and refrigerate for 30 minutes before serving.

Glace au Citron
FRANCE

Serves 4

Our testers agreed that this lemon ice was terrific, and so easy to make.

1	*juice and grated peel of a lemon*	*1*
1½ cups	*light cream*	*375 ml*
3	*egg yolks, well beaten*	*3*
½ cup	*sugar*	*125 ml*
⅛ tsp	*salt*	*pinch*

Grate lemon into cream which has been poured into medium saucepan. Add egg yolks, sugar and salt. Using a wire whisk, stir over low to medium heat for 7 minutes, or until mixture is the consistency of thin custard. Remove from heat, strain through a fine sieve and stir occasionally until lukewarm. Add strained lemon juice and stir to blend.

Pour mixture into metal ice-cube tray, cover with foil, and freeze for approximately 4 hours, stirring once or twice to prevent formation of large ice crystals.

This recipe can be successfully doubled.

Note:For a creamier texture, allow dessert to sit for 5 to 10 minutes at room temperature before serving.

Grapefruit Spread

BOTSWANA

Makes 2 cups/500 ml

Delicious on toast or scones or as a filling for tarts, this curd is easy to make and keeps well if refrigerated. In Botswana fresh juice and grated rind would be used.

1 cup	*frozen concentrated grapefruit juice, undiluted*	*250 ml*
3	*eggs, well beaten*	*3*
1/4 cup	*sugar*	*300 ml*
2 tsp	*unflavoured gelatine*	*10 ml*
1 tbsp	*water*	*15 ml*

Place grapefruit juice, eggs, butter and sugar in a medium saucepan. Bring slowly to boil, stirring contantly. Boil gently for 2 minutes. Sprinkle gelatine on water and dissolve over hot water before stirring into hot grapefruit mixture. Pour into hot sterilized jars. When cold, cover and refrigerate.

English Trifle
GREAT BRITAIN

Serves 6

The dictionary tells us "trifle" means of little importance - but this "trifle" is wonderful!

1	*sponge cake or pound cake*	*1*
⅓ cup	*raspberry jam*	*75 ml*
½ cup	*sherry*	*125 ml*
1	*15 oz package frozen raspberries, thawed*	*425 g*
2 cups	*vanilla custard*	*500 ml*
1 tsp	*vanilla*	*5 ml*
¼ tsp	*nutmeg*	*1 ml*
1 cup	*whipping cream*	*250 ml*
2	*macaroon cookies, crumbled*	*2*

Slice cake into ½ in/1.3 cm fingers; make into sandwiches, filling with jam. Arrange half the "sandwiches" in an attractive 2 qt/1 l bowl. Sprinkle with half the sherry. Repeat with remaining cake and sherry. Carefully spread raspberries over cake layers.

Prepare vanilla custard, allow it to cool slightly before adding vanilla and nutmeg. Pour over dessert. Press plastic wrap over custard to prevent a film from forming. Chill several hours to allow flavours to blend and mellow.

Remove from refrigerator 1 hour before serving. Top with whipped cream and sprinkle with crumbled macaroons.

Frozen Maple Mousse
QUEBEC

Serves 6 to 8

The delicate flavour of true maple syrup makes this dessert rich and delicious.

4	*large eggs at room temperature*	*4*
1 cup	*pure maple syrup*	*250 ml*
½ tsp	*vanilla*	*2 ml*
1 cup	*whipping cream*	*250 ml*

Separate eggs, putting whites in a medium mixing bowl. Place yolks and maple syrup in top of a double boiler. Stir to blend. Simmer until mixture thickens, approximately 15 to 18 minutes, stirring occasionally to prevent sticking. Remove from heat.

Add vanilla extract and whip with an electric mixer until cooled. Whip cream and fold in. Beat egg whites until stiff, and gently fold into cooled maple mixture. Spoon into 6 to 8 parfait glasses and freeze for 4 hours.

Remove from freezer 1 hour before serving.

Mandarin Snow Sponge

JAPAN

Serves 6 to 8

This layered dessert is sweet, light and airy.

1 tbsp	*unflavoured gelatine*	*15 ml*
½ cup	*cold water*	*125 ml*
1	*10 oz can mandarin oranges*	*284 ml*
1½ cups	*berry sugar*	*375 ml*
2	*egg whites*	*2*
1 tsp	*vanilla*	*5 ml*

Combine gelatine with water and set aside without stirring. Drain oranges, reserving juice. Set oranges aside. Add enough water to reserved juice to make 1½ cups/375 ml in total and place in a saucepan. Add softened gelatine and sugar, mixing well. Bring to the boil, stirring constantly, and continue to simmer gently for 7 minutes. Remove from heat and allow to cool to lukewarm.

Beat egg whites until very stiff. Slowly pour cooled syrup mixture into egg whites, while continuing to whip at medium speed. Fold in vanilla.

Pour mixture into a 9 in/23 cm square pan. Place oranges on top, in rows, and press down into mixture. Chill until set, at least 3 hours. To serve, cut into squares.

Oriental Custard

CHINA

Serves 6

Baked custard, chilled and served with a tasty fruit sauce.

4	*eggs*	*4*
1/4 cup	*sugar*	*50 ml*
1/4 tsp	*salt*	*1 ml*
1/2 tsp	*almond extract*	*2 ml*
3 cups	*milk, scalded*	*750 ml*
	boiling water	
1/3 cup	*sugar*	*75 ml*
1 tbsp	*cornstarch*	*15 ml*
2 cups	*orange juice*	*500 ml*
2 tsp	*orange peel, grated*	*10 ml*
1	*10 oz can mandarin oranges, drained*	*284 ml*
1	*8 oz can lichees or pineapple tidbits, drained*	*250 ml*

Preheat oven to 350°F/180°C.

Beat together eggs, sugar, salt and almond extract. Gradually beat in scalded milk.

Place six individual custard dishes in a deep baking pan. Pour equal amounts of custard into dishes. Pour boiling water around dishes, to reach the same level as the custard. Place in oven and bake about 20 minutes or until custard is set. Remove dishes, cool, cover and chill.

In a saucepan, combine 1/3 cup/75 ml sugar and cornstarch. Gradually blend in orange juice. Cook over medium heat, stirring until it boils and thickens. Remove from heat and stir in grated peel, oranges, and lichees or pineapple. Cool, cover and chill.

To serve, ladle orange mixture over cold custard.

Brandied Pears
HUNGARY

Serves 6

Sweet sherry or your favourite liqueur may be substituted for brandy in this special dessert.

1/3 cup	*brown sugar*	*75 ml*
1/3 cup	*water*	*75 ml*
1 tbsp	*fresh lemon juice*	*15 ml*
3	*large pears, peeled*	*3*
1/3 cup	*walnuts, finely chopped*	*75 ml*
2 tbsp	*brown sugar*	*30 ml*
1 1/2 tbsp	*brandy*	*22 ml*
1 tbsp	*plain yogurt*	*15 ml*
1 cup	*whipping cream*	*250 ml*
1 tbsp	*sugar*	*15 ml*
2 tsp	*brandy, sherry or liquer*	*10 ml*

Preheat oven to 325°F/165°C.

Mix 1/3 cup brown sugar, water and lemon juice and pour into an ungreased 9 in/23 cm baking pan. Cut pears in half, remove core. Arrange in pan, cut side down, and baste with sugar mixture. Cover and bake about 20 to 25 minutes until just tender when pierced with a fork.

Meanwhile, mix together nuts, sugar, brandy and yogurt, and set aside. Whip cream until fluffy, gradually sprinkling in remaining sugar. Add 2 tsp/10 ml brandy and finish whipping.

Place each pear half in serving dish and fill centre cavity with nut stuffing mixture. Serve warm, topped with flavoured whipped cream.

Rhubarb Kissel

U.S.S.R.

Serves 6

This versatile dessert can be made from an array of fresh, frozen or dried fruits. The amount of sugar will vary according to the tartness of the fruit.

1½ lbs	*rhubarb, sliced*	*750 g*
2 cups	*water*	*500 ml*
1 cup	*berry sugar*	*250 ml*
⅛ tsp	*salt*	*pinch*
3 tbsp	*cornstarch*	*45 ml*

Simmer rhubarb in water for 10 minutes, uncovered. Place in blender and purée. Mix sugar, salt and cornstarch in saucepan before gradually stirring in purée. Over low heat gradually bring to a boil and simmer about 2 minutes until mixture thickens, stirring constantly to prevent scorching. Cool slightly before pouring into dessert dishes.

Refrigerate for several hours before serving with heavy cream, ice cream or vanilla custard.

Rhubarb Strawberry Fantasy

ALBERTA

Serves 6

Fresh or frozen fruits can be used for this popular dessert.

3 cups	*rhubarb, chopped*	*750 ml*
1	*15 oz package sliced strawberries, thawed*	*425 g*
1 tbsp	*orange rind, grated*	*15 ml*
2 tbsp	*minute tapioca*	*30 ml*
3 cups	*corn flakes, crushed*	*750 ml*
⅔ cup	*sugar*	*175 ml*
¼ cup	*butter, melted*	*50 ml*

Preheat oven to 350°F/180°C.

Combine rhubarb, strawberries, orange rind and tapioca. In a separate bowl combine cornflake crumbs, sugar and butter. Place half the fruit in the bottom of a 1½ qt/1.5 l casserole. Sprinkle with half the crumb mixture. Repeat layers. Bake, uncovered, for 30 to 40 minutes. Serve with whipped cream or ice cream.

Tropical Fruit Salad
DOMINICAN REPUBLIC

Serves 6

Allow the flavours to blend and mellow by preparing this tropical fruit salad in advance.

1	*fresh pineapple, peeled and cubed*	*1*
2	*bananas, peeled and sliced*	*2*
2	*oranges, peeled and sectioned*	*2*
2	*cups melon, cubed*	*500 ml*
2	*mangos, cubed*	*2*
1 cup	*papaya, peeled and cubed*	*250 ml*
1 tsp	*sugar*	*5 ml*
1	*juice of 1 lemon*	*1*
½ cup	*fresh orange juice*	*125 ml*
⅓ cup	*light rum, cointreau or triple sec*	*75 ml*

Gently combine above ingredients in a large bowl. Chill for several hours before serving.

Note: For a variation add grapes, berries and apples.

Pavlova
AUSTRALIA

Serves 8

Soft meringue and passion fruit for a dessert beyond compare!

4	*large egg whites, at room temperature*	*4*
1 cup	*berry sugar*	*250 ml*
¼ cup	*granulated sugar*	*50 ml*
1 tbsp	*cornstarch*	*15 ml*
¼ tsp	*cream of tartar*	*1 ml*
1 tsp	*fresh lemon juice*	*5 ml*
1 cup	*whipping cream*	*250 ml*
	strawberries, some sliced, some whole	
	Kiwi fruit	
4	*passion fruit*	*4*
4 tsp	*berry sugar*	*20 ml*

Make meringue base the day before serving.

Preheat oven to 350°F/180°C.

Beat egg whites until stiff but not dry. Gradually add berry sugar, beating well after each addition, approximately 8 minutes. Combine granulated sugar, cornstarch and cream of tartar. Gently fold into meringue. Sprinkle with lemon juice and gently fold to finish blending. Meringue will now be smooth, stiff and glossy.

Place greaseproof paper or aluminum foil on a cookie sheet. Grease lightly and dust with flour, shaking off excess. Mark a 9 in/23 cm circle on paper and spread it with about half of meringue. Pipe remaining meringue around edge, using piping bag and wide star nozzle. If you have no piping bag, form Pavolva into a flan shape, higher around edges, flat in centre.

Place meringue in oven and immediately lower temperature to 250°F/120°C. Bake for 1 hour. Do not let it become brown. Turn oven off and allow meringue to cool in oven, preferably overnight. This step will avoid cracking.

Just before serving, whip cream and place in centre. Pour passion fruit pulp over top. Decorate with kiwi fruit, strawberries or other fresh fruit.

Note: Passion fruits, with their purple, wrinkled skins, are becoming more readily available. Cut in half, scoop out pulp and seeds, sweeten with 1 tsp/5 ml sugar per fruit.

Variation: Spread cooled meringue with the following lemon-cream filling to make use of the egg yolks left from the pavlova. Top with whipped cream and fresh fruits as above.

4	*large egg yolks*	*4*
¼ cup	*berry sugar*	*50 ml*
1 tsp	*vanilla*	*5 ml*
1 tbsp	*cornstarch*	*15 ml*
½ cup	*cream*	*125 ml*
¾ cup	*milk*	*200 ml*
	grated rind from 1 lemon	

Beat egg yolks, sugar, vanilla and cornstarch until smooth and creamy. Put into saucepan. Gradually add cream and milk and stir until smooth. Stir over medium heat until sauce thickens. Bring to boil, reduce heat and simmer for 2 minutes. Remove from heat, allow to cool, stirring occasionally. Fold in grated lemon rind.

Just before serving, pour cooled custard into meringue and decorate.

Fruit Meringue
NEW ZEALAND

Serves 6

Your favourite fruit and ice cream baked in meringue - a splendid dessert.

2	*bananas, peeled and sliced*	*2*
1	*kiwi fruit, peeled and sliced*	*1*
4	*medium egg whites, at room temperature*	*4*
¼ cup	*berry sugar*	*50 ml*
1 tsp	*vanilla*	*5 ml*
2 cups	*vanilla ice cream*	*500 ml*

Preheat oven to 400°F/205°C.

Place prepared fruit in a 9 in/23 cm pie plate and set in a larger pan filled with crushed ice. Set aside.

Whip egg whites until very stiff and dry, gradually adding sugar and vanilla. Cover fruit with ice cream and carefully spread meringue over entire surface of ice cream, extending right to edge to insulate from heat.

Place pie pan, still surrounded by crushed ice, in preheated oven for 5 to 7 minutes until meringue is golden brown.

Chestnut Soufflé
SPAIN

Serves 6 to 8

A special frozen soufflé - easily prepared with an electric mixer.

5	*large eggs, at room temperature*	*5*
2	*egg yolks, at room temperature*	*2*
⅔ cup	*sugar*	*175 ml*
2 tbsp	*gelatine*	*30 ml*
6 tbsp	*rum*	*90 ml*
1 cup	*unsweetened chestnut purée*	*250 ml*
1½ cups	*whipping cream*	*375 ml*
	marrons glacés or pistachio nuts to decorate	

Using an electric mixer, thoroughly beat eggs and yolks until thick and creamy, gradually adding sugar. Meanwhile, sprinkle gelatine over rum in a bowl, and place over hot water to dissolve. Do not stir until dissolved. Beat chestnut purée until very smooth and gradually add egg mixture, beating constantly. Beat in gelatine and rum. Whip cream and fold gently into mixture. Pour into prepared 6 cup/1.5 l soufflé dish and freeze until firm.

Remove from freezer 20 minutes before serving and garnish with additional whipped cream, marrons glacés or pistachio nuts.

Clearbrook Raspberry Soufflé
BRITISH COLUMBIA

Serves 8

Superb raspberries flavour a light soufflé.

¾ cup	*berry sugar*	*200 ml*
1½ cups	*water*	*375 ml*
4 cups	*fresh or frozen raspberries*	*1 l*
1½ tbsp	*unflavoured gelatine*	*15 g*
⅓ cup	*white wine*	*75 ml*
1½ cups	*whipping cream*	*375 ml*
5	*egg whites*	*5*
1 cup	*whipping cream*	*250 ml*
1 tbsp	*berry sugar*	*15 ml*

Place sugar and water in 2 qt/2 l saucepan, boil 5 minutes. Add raspberries, boil 5 more minutes. Purée mixture, then press through sieve to remove seeds. Return fruit to saucepan.

Blend gelatine and wine, add to saucepan. Heat gently until gelatine dissolves. Let mixture cool completely without setting.

Whip 1½ cups/375 ml cream, set aside. Beat egg whites until very stiff, set aside.

Place saucepan with raspberry mixture over ice. Beat with electric mixer until slightly jelled. Carefully fold in egg whites followed by whipped cream. Transfer into lightly oiled 2 qt/2 l soufflé dish. Cover with plastic wrap and refrigerate overnight.

To garnish, decorate with remaining cream which has been whipped with 1 tbsp/15 ml sugar. Just before serving complete garnish with a few whole raspberries.

Daiquiri Soufflé
PUERTO RICO

Serves 8

Heavenly!

10	*eggs, separated*	*10*
1 cup	*berry sugar*	*250 ml*
2	*juice and grated rind of 2 lemons*	*2*
2	*juice and grated rind of 2 limes*	*2*
1/8 tsp	*salt*	*pinch*
2 tbsp	*plain gelatine*	*30 ml*
1/2 cup	*white rum*	*125 ml*
2 cups	*whipping cream*	*500 ml*
1 cup	*whipping cream*	*250 ml*
	lime slices	
	crystallized violets	

In a medium saucepan, with a fork or wire whisk, beat egg yolks until light and fluffy. Gradually add sugar and continue beating until smooth and light in colour. Add lime and lemon juice, grated rinds and pinch of salt. Mix thoroughly. Stir over low heat until mixture thickens.

Soak gelatine in rum, then stir into hot custard, blending until gelatine is dissolved. Cool until lukewarm.

In one bowl, beat egg whites until stiff and in another bowl whip 2 cups/500 ml whipping cream. Fold egg whites into custard. Fold in whipped cream. Carefully transfer mixture into a soufflé dish or fancy glass bowl. Chill overnight in the refrigerator.

To serve, whip remaining cream. Decorate top of soufflé with whipped cream rosettes, crystallized violets and lime slices.

Note: This dessert freezes well.

Apricot Flan
EAST GERMANY

Serves 6 to 8

Glazed apricots in an almond flavoured shortbread - mmm!

Shortbread base:

½ cup	*butter, at room temperature*	*125 ml*
½ cup	*berry sugar*	*125 ml*
1	*egg*	*1*
1 tsp	*vanilla*	*5 ml*
½ tsp	*almond extract*	*2 ml*
1 cup	*flour*	*250 ml*
1 tsp	*baking powder*	*5 ml*
1 tbsp	*flour*	*15 ml*

Fruit layer:

⅔ cup	*apricot jam*	*175 ml*
1	*19 oz can apricot halves, drained (reserve syrup)*	*540 ml*

Glaze:

⅓ oz	*package of glaze powder for fresh fruit tarts*	*10 g*
1 cup	*apricot syrup (from can)*	*250 ml*

Preheat oven to 375°F/195°C.

Cream together butter and sugar. Add egg, almond extract and vanilla and cream until smooth. Sift together 1 cup/250 ml flour and baking powder and add to butter mixture. Press about ⅔ cup of above mixture into bottom of 9 in/23 cm springform pan. To remaining ⅓ cup of mixture, add 1 tbsp/15 ml flour and mix. Roll into a cylinder and place around inside of pan to form an edge to hold in apricots. Crimp edge decoratively. Prick bottom with a fork.

Bake for approximately 25 minutes or until edges of pastry are golden brown. Cool.

Spread cooled crust with jam and arrange apricots on top, cut side down. Combine glaze powder and apricot syrup in small saucepan. Cook over medium heat, stirring constantly until mixture thickens and comes to a boil. Allow to cool 1 minute, then pour over cake, starting from centre.

Cool completely, and store in refrigerator until 15 minutes before serving time.

Coconut Cream Pie

LIBERIA

Serves 8

In Africa, freshly grated coconut would be used for this rich but easy-to-make pie.

	pastry to line a 9 in/23 cm pie plate	
3 tbsp	*berry sugar*	*45 ml*
1¼ cups	*shredded coconut, unsweetened*	*300 ml*
1 tsp	*vanilla extract*	*5 ml*
¼ tsp	*salt*	*1 ml*
½ tsp	*nutmeg, grated*	*2 ml*
1½ cups	*milk*	*375 ml*
3	*egg yolks, beaten*	*3*

Preheat oven to 450°F/230°C.

Line pie plate with pastry. Combine remaining ingredients and turn into pastry case. Bake for 10 minutes. Reduce heat to 350°F/180°C, and bake a further 35 minutes until filling has set. Cool.

Topping:

3	*egg whites*	*3*
¼ tsp	*cream of tartar*	*1 ml*
¼ cup	*berry sugar*	*50 ml*
½ tsp	*vanilla extract*	*2 ml*
	glacé cherries to decorate	

Preheat oven to 300°F/150°C.

Beat egg whites and cream of tartar until stiff. Continue beating while gradually adding sugar and vanilla. Spread over cooled pie. Return to oven for 12 to 15 minutes until lightly browned.

Chiffon Pumpkin Pie Supreme

UNITED STATES OF AMERICA

Serves 8

This delicious pumpkin pie has a surprise middle layer of delicately spiced whipped cream.

Base:

1½ cups	*ginger snap cookie crumbs*	*375ml*
⅛ tsp	*ground ginger*	*pinch*
¼ cup	*melted butter*	*50 ml*

Filling:

1 tbsp	*unflavoured gelatine*	*15 ml*
⅓ cup	*sugar*	*75 ml*
¼ tsp	*salt*	*1 ml*
½ tsp	*cinnamon*	*2 ml*
½ tsp	*allspice*	*2 ml*
¼ tsp	*ginger*	*1 ml*
¼ tsp	*nutmeg*	*2 ml*
½ cup	*milk*	*125 ml*
3	*egg yolks, beaten*	*3*
1 cup	*canned pumpkin*	*250 ml*
3	*egg whites*	*3*
¼ cup	*sugar*	*50 ml*

Middle layer:

1 cup	*whipped cream*	*250 ml*
¼ cup	*icing sugar*	*50 ml*
½ tsp	*vanilla*	*2 ml*
¼ tsp	*cinnamon*	*1 ml*

Preheat oven to 350°F/180°C.

Base: Combine cookie crumbs, ginger and butter. Press into a 9 in/23 cm pie plate. Bake for 10 minutes. Set aside to cool.

Filling: In a medium saucepan, combine gelatine, ⅓ cup/75 ml sugar, salt and spices. Stir in milk, egg yolks and pumpkin. Cook, stirring, over medium heat until mixture boils and gelatine has dissolved. Remove from heat. Cool, and chill until partially set.

Beat egg whites until soft peaks form. Gradually add remaining sugar and beat for several minutes longer until peaks are stiff. Gently fold egg whites into cooled pumpkin mixture and pile half into cooled pie crust.

Middle Layer: Combine whipped cream, icing sugar, vanilla and remaining cinnamon and whip until soft peaks form. Gently spread half this mixture over the pumpkin in pie shell. Carefully top with remaining pumpkin and chill about 2 hours or until firm.
To serve: Using the remaining whipped cream mixture, pipe rosettes on top of pie to decorate.

Saskatchewan Fruit Pie

SASKATCHEWAN

Serves 6 to 8

Make this superb pie any time of year, using fresh or frozen fruit.

	pastry to line a deep 10 in/26 cm pie pan	
¾ cup	*golden sugar*	*200 ml*
1 cup	*light cream*	*250 ml*
1 tsp	*vanilla*	*5 ml*
2 tbsp	*flour*	*30 ml*
1 cup	*cranberries, fresh or frozen*	*250 ml*
2 cups	*apples, peeled and sliced*	*500 ml*
½ cup	*seedless raisins*	*125 ml*
1 tbsp	*butter*	*15 ml*
¼ cup	*walnuts, chopped*	*50 ml*
2 tbsp	*sugar*	*30 ml*

Preheat oven to 375°F/190°C.

Line the pie pan with pastry. In a medium saucepan combine golden sugar and cream. Heat gently, stirring until sugar dissolves. Cool, and add vanilla. Measure flour into a large bowl, gradually stirring cream mixture into the flour. Add all fruit and stir to blend. Turn into pie shell. Dot with butter and walnuts, and sprinkle with sugar. Cover with strips of pastry.

Bake for 40 to 45 minutes. Serve warm.

Butter Tarts Supreme
ALBERTA

Makes 12

The best ever!

	plain pastry to line 12, 3 in/7.5 cm tart pans	
½ cup	*seedless raisins*	*125 ml*
	boiling water	
¼ cup	*butter*	*50 ml*
½ cup	*brown sugar*	*125 ml*
¼ tsp	*salt*	*1 ml*
½ cup	*golden corn syrup*	*125 ml*
1	*egg*	*1*
1 tsp	*vanilla*	*5 ml*

Preheat oven to 450°F/230°C.

Line tart pans with pastry.

Cover raisins with boiling water and let stand for a few minutes before draining. Do not pat dry. Mix still warm raisins with butter, sugar, salt and corn syrup, and stir till butter and sugar are dissolved. Add egg and vanilla, stir well, and spoon into pastry lined pans.

Place in oven, and immediately lower temperature to 400°F/200°C. Bake 15 to 20 minutes, or until filling is bubbling and nicely browned. Loosen tarts, but do not remove from pans until thoroughly cool.

Lemon Squares
NOVA SCOTIA

Makes 9 squares

Serve this refreshing sweet at the end of a hearty meal or as a tea-time snack.

Base:

½ cup	*butter or margarine*	*125 ml*
½ cup	*sugar*	*125 ml*
1½ cups	*flour*	*375 ml*
½ tsp	*salt*	*2 ml*
1 tsp	*baking powder*	*5 ml*

Filling:

1	*juice and rind of a lemon*	*1*
2	*egg yolks (reserve whites)*	*2*
1 tbsp	*butter*	*15 ml*
¾ cup	*sugar*	*200 ml*
1½ tbsp	*cornstarch*	*22 ml*
1 cup	*hot water*	*250 ml*

Topping:

2	*egg whites*	*2*
¼ cup	*sugar*	*50 ml*

Preheat oven to 375°F/190°C.

In a medium bowl combine butter, sugar, flour, salt and baking powder. Pat crumbly mixture into an 8 in/20 cm square pan, saving ¼ cup for topping. Bake for 12 to 15 minutes. Cool.

Combine filling ingredients in a saucepan. Place over medium heat and cook, stirring constantly, until mixture thickens, about 7 minutes. Cool slightly. Pour filling over cooled base.

Beat egg whites and sugar until stiff. Spread over filling to cover completely. Sprinkle reserved crumbs over all, return to oven, and brown about 5 minutes. Cool slightly before slicing.

West German Cheesecake

WEST GERMANY

Serves 8

This is a traditional cheese cake with an unexpected texture.

Pastry:

1¼ cups	*flour*	*300 ml*
½ cup	*butter*	*125 ml*
¼ cup	*icing sugar*	*50 ml*
¼ cup	*ground almonds*	*50 ml*
⅛ tsp	*salt*	*pinch*
1	*egg, beaten*	*1*

Filling:

1½ cup	*baking cheese*	*375 ml*
¼ cup	*butter, softened*	*50 ml*
¼ cup	*ground almonds*	*50 ml*
½ cup	*icing sugar*	*125 ml*
1 tbsp	*fresh lemon peel*	*15 ml*
2 tsp	*fresh lemon juice*	*10 ml*
3	*eggs, beaten*	*3*
¾ cup	*currants or raisins*	*200 ml*
1	*egg, beaten*	*1*
1 tbsp	*icing sugar*	*15 ml*

Preheat oven to 375°F/190°C.

Sift flour into a bowl, cut in butter and work mixture until as fine as breadcrumbs. Add sugar, almonds and salt and continue to blend. Add beaten egg and mix with a fork until a ball of moist, not sticky, dough is formed.

Chill for 30 minutes before rolling out on a lightly floured board. Line a 10 in/25.5 cm pie pan, reserving some pastry for a lattice work topping. Bake empty pie shell for 10 minutes.

Filling: Combine first 7 ingredients, mixing thoroughly. Sprinkle currants or raisins evenly over baked pie shell. Spoon in cheese mixture. Decorate pie with strips of pastry, forming a lattice pattern.

Bake at same temperature for 30 to 35 minutes. Brush beaten egg on filling for last 5 minutes of baking time to give a glossy look.

Cool pie, and sprinkle with icing sugar before serving.

P.E.I. Chocolate Cake

PRINCE EDWARD ISLAND

Makes 18 pieces

The addition of mashed potatoes gives a light, moist texture to this family favourite. Flavour improves if made a day in advance.

1 cup	*butter or margarine, at room temperature*	*250 ml*
2 cups	*sugar*	*500 ml*
4	*medium eggs*	*4*
3	*squares unsweetened chocolate, melted*	*84 g*
1 cup	*mashed potatoes, cold*	*250 ml*
¼ tsp	*nutmeg*	*1 ml*
1 tsp	*cinnamon*	*5 ml*
1	*grated rind of an orange*	*1*
2 cups	*flour*	*500 ml*
1 tsp	*baking soda*	*5 ml*
1 cup	*buttermilk*	*250 ml*
½ cup	*walnuts, chopped*	*125 ml*

Preheat oven to 350°F/180°C.

In a large mixing bowl, cream butter or margarine. Gradually add sugar, and with an electric mixer beat until light and fluffy. Add eggs, one at a time, beating well after each addition. Add melted chocolate, potato, spices and orange rind.

Sift flour and baking soda together. Add to chocolate mixture alternately with buttermilk. Beat well. Fold in chopped walnuts.

Pour into a greased and floured 9 x 13 in/3.5 l cake pan. Bake 50 to 60 minutes, or until cake tester comes out clean. Cool for 1 hour in pan before inverting on a rack to cool completely.

Top with your favourite orange or chocolate flavoured icing.

Mandel Torte
SWITZERLAND

Serves 8

A festive-looking almond pastry to serve as dessert, or at coffee time.

Pastry:

1¼ cups	*flour*	*300 ml*
1 tsp	*baking powder*	*5 ml*
5 tbsp	*berry sugar*	*75 ml*
½ cup	*soft butter*	*125 ml*
1	*egg, lightly beaten*	*1*

Filling:

½ cup	*soft butter*	*125 ml*
½ cup	*berry sugar*	*125 ml*
1 cup	*almonds, finely ground*	*250 ml*
½ tsp	*almond extract*	*2 ml*
2	*eggs*	*2*

Topping:

½ cup	*raspberry jam*	*125 ml*
	candied red & green cherries, halved	
4 tbsp	*icing sugar*	*60 ml*
2 tsp	*fresh lemon juice*	*10 ml*

Sift flour, baking powder and sugar into a bowl, and thoroughly mix in butter and egg. Work dough until it forms a ball.

Press into greased 9 in/23 cm springform pan, covering bottom and 1 in/2.5 cm up sides. Cover and chill for 30 minutes.

Preheat oven to 350°F/180°C.

Beat all filling ingredients together until light. Spread in pastry shell. Bake in preheated oven for about 50 minutes, or until pastry is golden and filling is set. Cool for 1 hour.

Spread with raspberry jam and decorate with red and green cherry halves. Refrigerate for 15 to 20 minutes.

Mix icing sugar with a little lemon juice, then drizzle thin lines of icing amongst the cherries.

Sachertorte
AUSTRIA

Serves 12

An Austrian tradition, this rich chocolate cake is always served with freshly whipped cream.

6 oz	*semi-sweet chocolate, in small pieces*	*140 g*
8	*medium egg yolks*	*8*
1 cup	*unsalted butter, melted*	*250 ml*
1 tsp	*vanilla*	*5 ml*
10	*medium egg whites*	*10*
⅛ tsp	*salt*	*pinch*
¾ cup	*berry sugar*	*200 ml*
1 cup	*flour*	*250 ml*
⅓ cup	*apricot jam*	*75 ml*
2 tsp	*apricot brandy*	*10 ml*

Glaze:

3 oz	*unsweetened chocolate, in small pieces*	*75 g*
1 cup	*whipping cream, unwhipped*	*250 ml*
1 cup	*berry sugar*	*250 ml*
1 tsp	*light corn syrup*	*5 ml*
1	*egg*	*1*
1 tsp	*vanilla*	*5 ml*

Preheat oven to 350°F/180°C.

Line the bottoms of two 9 in/23 cm round cake pans with circles of greased paper.

Melt chocolate in top of double boiler, stirring occasionally with wooden spoon. In a small mixing bowl, break up egg yolks. Beat in melted chocolate, butter and vanilla.

In a large bowl beat egg whites and a pinch of salt until stiff. Add berry sugar, a tablespoon at a time. Continue to beat until egg whites form stiff unwavering peaks. Blend about ⅓ of the egg whites thoroughly into yolk-chocolate mixture. Pour this mixture carefully over remaining egg whites. Sprinkle the cup of flour over the top, and with a large slotted spoon gently fold together until no trace of whites or flour remain. Do not overmix.

Pour batter evenly into the two prepared pans. Bake approximately 30 minutes, or until a cake tester comes out clean. Remove pans from oven. Allow to sit for 15 minutes before loosening, and a further 15 minutes before turning out. When completely cool, mix apricot jam with brandy and spread between layers. Place cake on wire rack on cookie sheet.

Glaze: In a small saucepan, combine chocolate, cream, sugar and corn syrup. Stirring constantly with a wooden spoon, cook over low heat until melted. Raise heat to medium and cook without stirring for 15 to 20 minutes or until syrup reaches soft ball stage.

In a small mixing bowl, mix the egg with four tablespoons of the hot chocolate syrup. Pour this into remaining chocolate in saucepan. Remove from heat, add vanilla, and stir until blended. Carefully pour warm glaze over cake, ensuring that sides are completely covered by using a spatula or knife dipped in hot water. The glaze sets quickly, so work fast. Do not touch glaze again until it is set, as this spoils the gloss.

Refrigerate cake for 3 hours. Serve with whipped cream.

Variation: To make individual Sachertortes, cut cake into 12 portions before covering with glaze. To finish, the "sacher" signature can be dribbled on with a pointed knife dipped in hot glaze.

Vinaterta
MANITOBA

Serves 6 to 8

This dessert recipe must be made a day ahead to allow the filling and flavours to soak through the cake layers. If wrapped and stored in the refrigerator, it will keep for 2 weeks.

Dough:

1 cup	*butter, melted*	*250 ml*
1½ cups	*sugar*	*375 ml*
2	*eggs*	*2*
2 tbsp	*light cream*	*30 ml*
1 tbsp	*almond extract*	*15 ml*
4 cups	*flour*	*1 l*
1 tsp	*baking powder*	*5 ml*
1 tsp	*cardamom or cinnamon*	*5 ml*

In a large bowl, cream butter and sugar together, using a wire whisk or electric mixer. Beat in eggs, one at a time. Add cream and extract; beat again. Mix together flour, baking powder and cardamom or cinnamon. Blend gradually into creamed mixture.

Preheat oven to 375°F/190°C.

Knead dough on a floured board 20 times. Divide dough into 7 equal portions. Pat each portion into a 9 in/23 cm greased layer cake pan, lined with waxed paper and bake for 10 to 12 minutes or until golden brown. Remove from pan and peel off paper while still hot. Cool. Put layers together with prune filling. If desired, ice with your favourite almond or vanilla butter icing. Whipped cream is also delicious with this originally Icelandic dessert.

Prune Filling:

2 cups	*pitted prunes*	*500 ml*
1¼ cups	*water*	*300 ml*
1 cup	*sugar*	*250 ml*
⅔ cup	*liquid reserved from stewing prunes*	*175 ml*
1 tbsp	*cinnamon*	*15 ml*
1 tsp	*vanilla*	*5 ml*

Cover prunes with water in heavy saucepan. Bring to boil. Boil 10 minutes, stirring frequently. Drain, reserving ⅔ cup/175 ml liquid. Put prunes through blender or food processor. Return prune purée to saucepan and add sugar, reserved liquid and cinnamon. Bring to boil and cook for another 10 minutes.

When cool, stir in vanilla and spread on the cake layers.

Swedish Spritz Cookies

SWEDEN

Makes 3 to 4 dozen

A traditional Christmas treat, these cookies are just too good to be served only at Christmas time.

½ cup	*butter*	*125 ml*
½ cup	*margarine*	*125 ml*
⅔ cup	*berry sugar*	*175 ml*
1	*egg, beaten*	*1*
½ tsp	*vanilla*	*2 ml*
½ tsp	*almond extract*	*2 ml*
2½ cups	*flour*	*550 ml*
½ tsp	*baking powder*	*2 ml*
¼ tsp	*salt*	*1 ml*
	red or green food colouring, optional	
	red or green maraschino cherries	
1 oz	*semi-sweet chocolate*	*25 g*

Preheat oven to 375°F/190°C.

Cream butter and margarine until light; gradually add sugar. Combine beaten egg with vanilla and almond extract. Add to creamed mixture, blending well. Sift flour, baking powder and salt together; add to butter-sugar mixture and stir until well blended. Tint dough if desired.

Using a cookie press or pastry bag, press dough into a variety of shapes and on an ungreased cookie sheet bake for 10 to 12 minutes.

Note: Traditional shapes are rosebuds decorated with cherry before cooking, and logs and wreaths dipped in melted chocolate when cooked and cooled.

Scandinavian Kringler

DENMARK

Makes 16 slices

Kringler, a Christmas almond pastry, is easy to prepare for any occasion.

Base:

1 cup	*flour*	*250 ml*
1/8 tsp	*salt*	*pinch*
1/2 cup	*butter, chilled*	*125 ml*
2 tbsp	*ice-water*	*30 ml*

Puff Topping:

1 cup	*water*	*250 ml*
1/2 cup	*butter*	*125 ml*
1 cup	*flour*	*250 ml*
3	*eggs*	*3*
1/2 tsp	*almond extract*	*2 ml*
1/8 tsp	*salt*	*pinch*

Icing:

1 1/4 cups	*icing sugar*	*300 ml*
1 tbsp	*butter, at room temperature*	*15 ml*
1/2 tsp	*almond extract*	*2 ml*
3 tbsp	*milk*	*45 ml*
2 tbsp	*slivered almonds*	*30 ml*

Base: Measure flour and salt into mixing bowl. Using a pastry blender, cut in chilled butter until particles resemble peas. Sprinkle with ice-water, a little at a time, mixing lightly with a fork until a soft dough forms. This base can also be prepared in a food processor. Divide dough in half. On an ungreased cookie sheet, press each half into 12 in/30 cm x 3 in/7.5 cm strips.

Puff Topping: Combine water and butter in medium saucepan. Bring to boil over medium heat. Remove from heat, immediately stir in 1 cup/250 ml flour and beat until smooth. Add eggs, one at a time, beating for at least 3 minutes after each addition. Add extract and salt and stir vigorously for a further 2 minutes. Spoon dough over two crusts, spreading to within 1/2 in/1.3 cm from edges.

Bake for 65 to 75 minutes, until golden brown and puffy. Cool.

Icing: Blend icing sugar, butter, almond extract and milk until smooth. Spoon over cooled kringler and sprinkle with slivered almonds.

Kourabiedes
GREECE

Makes 36

Kourabiedes are a delicious "melt-in-your-mouth" shortbread cookie.

1 cup	*butter, at room temperature*	*250 ml*
½ cup	*icing sugar, sifted*	*125 ml*
1	*egg yolk*	*1*
1 tsp	*vanilla*	*5 ml*
2 tsp	*ouzo, brandy, or amaretto*	*10 ml*
2 cups	*flour*	*500 ml*
¼ tsp	*salt*	*1 ml*
½ cup	*almonds, finely chopped*	*125 ml*
¼ cup	*icing sugar*	*50 ml*

Preheat oven to 350°F/180°C.

Cream butter and sugar until light and fluffy; add egg yolk, vanilla and liqueur. Blend well. Stir in flour, salt and ground almonds. Roll small amounts of dough into logs and shape into crescents. Place on an ungreased cookie sheet. Bake for 10 to 12 minutes.

Cookies will brown slightly on the bottom, but remain very pale on top. Remove to wire rack and sift icing sugar over top while cookies are still warm.

Pastelitos de Dulce
ARGENTINA

Makes approximately 25

Deep fried pastries are a traditional sweet in Argentina — well worth the effort.

3½ cups	*flour*	*875 ml*
½ cup	*butter, chilled*	*125 ml*
½ tsp	*salt*	*2 ml*
¼ cup	*ice water*	*50 ml*
2	*egg yolks*	*2*
¼ cup	*butter, melted and cooled*	*50 ml*
	flour	
¾ cup	*"dulce de membrillo" (quince jam)*	*200 ml*
	vegetable shortening for deep frying	
1 cup	*sugar*	*250 ml*
¼ cup	*water*	*50 ml*
½ tsp	*vanilla*	*2 ml*
	multi-coloured trimettes to decorate	

In large mixing bowl mix flour, chilled butter and salt until well blended. Beat water and egg yolks together and add to flour mixture, a quarter at a time. Work pastry until a ball of dough is formed.

Place dough on a lightly floured surface and knead about 5 minutes until dough is smooth and elastic. With a floured rolling pin, roll dough into a 12 in/30 cm square.

Brush pastry with some of the melted butter and sprinkle lightly with flour. Smooth surface of dough with palms of hands until flour absorbs butter and surface looks dry. Fold dough in half and repeat above process 3 more times until you have a 3 in/7.5 cm square. Roll dough into a 14 in/35 cm square. Measure and cut into 49, 2 in/5 cm squares.

In centre of half the squares, place 1 tsp/5 ml quince jam. Moisten dough around filling with cold water and pair with remaining squares, pressing dough firmly around filling to seal.

Pour oil into two heavy saucepans or deep fryers to a depth of 2 in/5 cm. Simultaneously heat one pan of fat to 375°F/190°C and the other to 175°F/80°C. Drop as many pastelitos as pan will comfortably hold into the 175°F/80°C fat and fry for 3 minutes. Do not brown. Immediately transfer with a slotted spoon to the pan of 375°F/190°C fat and fry, turning frequently until golden brown. With tongs, remove from fat and drain on paper towels.

Syrup: Combine sugar and water in small saucepan. Bring to boil, stirring constantly. Turn down heat and keep warm. Dip pastelitos in syrup and place on waxed paper to cool. To decorate, sprinkle both sides with trimettes immediately after dipping.

Note: For savoury pastelitos, fill with cooked meat or seafood and serve hot or cold as hors d'oeuvres. The sweet syrup is omitted.

Spence Bay Coffee-Rum Sauce
NORTHWEST TERRITORIES

Serves 6 to 8

Quick and easy! Serve with ice cream.

2 tbsp	*instant coffee powder*	*30 ml*
½ cup	*water*	*125 ml*
2 tbsp	*icing sugar*	*30 ml*
1 cup	*light cream*	*250 ml*
½ cup	*whipping cream*	*125 ml*
½ tsp	*vanilla*	*2 ml*
1	*3¼ oz package instant vanilla pudding mix*	*92 g*
3 oz	*dark rum (more if you prefer!)*	*75 ml*
1 qt	*vanilla or coffee ice cream*	*1 l*
	dessert wafers	

Dissolve instant coffee in water. Add sugar and stir until dissolved. Add cream, whipping cream, vanilla and pudding mix. Stir until well blended. Let mixture set for 5 minutes. Gradually stir in rum. Chill thoroughly.

To serve, place scoops of ice cream in parfait glasses. Generously top with coffee-rum sauce, and serve with dessert wafers.

Variation: Combine in a blender or food processor equal amounts of slightly softened ice cream with coffee-rum sauce and whirl to blend. Spoon mixture into parfait glasses and freeze for approximately 4 hours. Remove from freezer 5 minutes before serving.

INDEX

LET'S COOK INTERNATIONAL ORDER FORM

Please send ______ copies of Let's Cook International @ $9.95 each plus $1 postage and handling.

Total amount enclosed ______________________________

Mail to: Name ______________________________

Address ______________________________

City ______________________ Province ______________

Postal Code ______________________________

Make cheque or money order payable to:

Let's Cook International
The Canadian Red Cross Society,
B.C./Yukon Division,
4750 Oak Street,
Vancouver, B.C., V6H 2N9

This price valid until December 31st, 1986

LET'S COOK INTERNATIONAL ORDER FORM

Please send ______ copies of Let's Cook International @ $9.95 each plus $1 postage and handling.

Total amount enclosed ______________________________

Mail to: Name ______________________________

Address ______________________________

City ____________________ Province ______________

Postal Code ______________________________

Make cheque or money order payable to:

Let's Cook International
The Canadian Red Cross Society,
B.C./Yukon Division,
4750 Oak Street,
Vancouver, B.C., V6H 2N9

This price valid until December 31st, 1986